The Kogan Page Market Research Series breaks new ground in market research publishing. While most books tend to be all-embracing tomes covering every aspect of market research, each title in this new series is d   r key area.

The prime aim of the ti   y the technicalities of market rese   _stible introductions, presented in a clear and comprehensive style.

Well-illustrated throughout, these practical guides will serve as vital introductions for those new to market research, useful revision tools for students and essential refreshers for all market research professionals.

Titles in the series are:

> *Questionnaire Design*
> *Interviewing*
> *Sampling and Statistics*

Future titles will cover:

> Desk research
> Reporting and presenting data
> Analysis and modelling

ABOUT THE AUTHORS

■

Paul Hague is a Chairman of Business and Market Research PLC. He regularly contributes to the market research trade press and lectures at seminars on the subject. He is author of *The Industrial Market Research Handbook* and co-author of *Do Your Own Market Research, How to do Marketing Research* and *Market Research in Practice*. He is also joint editor of *A Handbook of Market Research Techniques*. All these books are published by Kogan Page.

Paul Harris is a Director of Statistical Services at MAI Research Ltd (formerly NOP), a position he has held for 25 years. He writes and lectures widely on various topics for the Market Research Society and other bodies.

SAMPLING and STATISTICS

Paul Hague and Paul Harris

KOGAN PAGE

041175

First published in 1993

Kogan Page Limited
120 Pentonville Road
London N1 9JN

© Paul Hague and Paul Harris, 1993

British Library Cataloguing in Publication Data

A CIP record for this book is available from the British Library.

ISBN 0 7494 0916 9

Typeset by BookEns Limited, Baldock, Herts.
Printed in England by Clays Ltd, St Ives Plc.

CONTENTS

■

PREFACE

∎

Much market research data consists of numbers, and statistics is the science of numbers. It is not, therefore, surprising that the analysis and interpretation of market research data involves using statistical theory. This does not mean that all market researchers necessarily have to be trained statisticians — in fact very few are — but it does mean that market researchers should be aware of basic statistical concepts.

The main areas on which researchers should have an understanding are related to the measurement and variability of data collected from sample surveys. They should know how to summarise the numerical data collected from surveys and how to assess their accuracy. They should be aware of the effect of sample size on accuracy and be able to distinguish between real changes measured by surveys as opposed to random fluctuations caused by sampling variability. And, since market research often seeks to answer questions about the future, so too the researcher should have a general understanding about forecasting.

The book begins with a brief introduction to the market research process and then introduces some basic statistical concepts on measurement and dispersion. The centrepiece of the book is sampling. Whereas researchers can lean on computers for instant answers on statistical tests, they must have a firm grasp of the principles of finding out a lot from a little if they are to make their way in the quantitative side of our profession. The final chapters in the book introduce the subject of forecasting where we look at the application of correlation and time series.

This book is intended as a taster. It aims to give researchers the rudiments of knowledge on key issues in sampling and data control and hopefully to whet the appetite to dig deeper and read wider.

Paul Hague and Paul Harris
January 1993

1

FACING A MOUNTAIN OF DATA

■

MARKET RESEARCH AND DECISION MAKING

Market research (sometimes referred to as marketing research) is the collection of information to guide marketing decisions. Most people on the commercial side of business would say that, according to this definition, everyone is a market researcher because they wouldn't dream of making a serious decision without some information. However, market research implies that the collection activity is a systematic approach and that somewhere in the process a survey is involved. Of course, information gathering can take place without a survey and desk research (by which we mean the analysis of published information) is also an important input into the data pot.

Market research surveys range from small qualitative studies involving just a handful of people through to large quantitative studies in which hundreds, even thousands, of people are interviewed. This book offers guidance to the market researcher who has to design, control and interpret the data from quantitative surveys.

The survey data will not itself be the only input in the decision-making process. Managers will consider the results of the survey against a company's resources, its present performance, financial analyses and the like. Nevertheless, in some shape or form the market research work will guide decisions to:

- plan the future for an existing product or service;
- invest in new capacity to supply a product or service;
- enter a new market, either a new sector or an export territory;
- sharpen the effectiveness of a promotional programme;
- beat off the competition (whether a company or a political party);
- acquire a company.

THE FOUR INGREDIENTS OF QUALITY MARKET RESEARCH

Information which is as portentous as that which will guide the above decisions must be right. In fact no information at all is better than bad information since the latter could lead a company down the wrong path and towards disaster. Quality market research is the result of care and attention to four vital aspects of the process:

1. Asking the right question

Surveys are driven by questionnaires — the lists of questions asked of people. The questions on a questionnaire must be tightly designed to ensure that:

— there is no ambiguity in any of the words or the questions;
— questions are not loaded or biased in any way;
— questions are within the scope and capability of the respondents;
— questions are relevant to the subject;
— there are no missing questions.

These points seem obvious but even experienced market researchers know to their cost that, sometimes with the greater knowledge gained from carrying out a survey, it becomes clear exactly what questions should have been asked at the time of data analysis. Having 20/20 vision when designing the questionnaire, knowing what should be asked and how to ask it, is one of the fundamentals of good quality market research.

There is another book in this series which will give the reader greater insights into questionnaire design.*

2.   Finding the right person

It is no good designing the perfect questionnaire and then asking the questions of the wrong person. Market research interviewers are trained and skilled in the task of finding the right people and asking questions. At the heart of this subject is *sampling* which we cover in detail in this book.

Sampling allows market researchers to collect data from only a proportion of the targeted respondents and to draw wider conclusions based on the results of that sample. Without samples, market research surveys would be impractical and too costly. Very often the interviewer is given a *quota* which is a statement of the number and type of people that they should interview. The instruction may simply state that 'X' number of respondents of a certain age, social class and sex are required. Since these interviews are undertaken largely in the home or on the street, a considerable responsibility lies on the shoulders of the interviewer to make sure that the correct people are chosen. Bias could be introduced into a survey if, for example:

■   the respondents all come from the same street or know each other (resulting in localised bias);

■   the respondents are known to the interviewer (creating bias in sensitive questions as respondents could disguise answers to avoid disclosing personal details to their acquaintance, the interviewer);

■   the respondents come from the marketing industry (causing them to 'second guess' the reasons for the questions or even, by chance, having prior knowledge of the purpose of the survey).

For these reasons most surveys have tight requirements on the type of person that can be interviewed and there are often special questions at the start of the questionnaire to screen out people who should be excluded.

---

* Hague, P (1993) *Questionnaire Design*, Kogan Page, London

Along with the requirement to obtain suitable respondents, it is behoven on the interviewer to ask the question *exactly* as it is written on the questionnaire. Any slight deviation from a question could result in answers skewed by the variation in the way it was asked. This would not necessarily be apparent to the researchers attempting to analyse the results and the data could therefore be misinterpreted. Equally it goes without saying that the interviewer must record exactly what the respondent says. In the case of large surveys most questions are pre-coded; this means that the interviewer only has to circle a number against one of the listed answers. If there is an open-ended question, in which the respondent is free to say what they like, then the interviewer must capture the true essence of the response even if it is not exactly verbatim.

Since most interviewing is done out of sight of the market researchers controlling the survey, there must be checks to ensure that it is carried out correctly. It is normal to take a 10 per cent sample of each interviewer's work and recontact respondents for two purposes. First, and most importantly, to ensure that the interview was actually carried out, and secondly to include a limited number of control questions as a check against what was actually recorded at the time of the interview.

3. Analysing the data

Once the right question has been asked of the right person, the data must be analysed. For this purpose the questionnaires are returned to the market research company where they are checked and edited to see that all the questions have been asked and the responses are legible.

The questionnaires now move into the data processing department where coders reduce the open-ended questions to a manageable list of response categories with appropriate numbers suitable for punching into the computers. Here again quality becomes an issue as the open response must be distilled into the correct code and for this a degree of interpretation is required. As the data is entered into computers, more quality checks are needed to ensure that the task is performed accurately. Market research software, which carries out the cross analysis, performs logic checks to indicate if data has been entered against inappropriate questions while the accuracy of data entry is validated by a proportion of work being double punched.

As the last part of the data analysis process, a specification is prepared to instruct the market research software on weighting, filtering and cross analysis.

4. Interpreting the data

The fourth and final part of the market research process is interpretation of the data. Here the market researchers are looking for patterns of response for each question but also comparing and contrasting the findings from different groups of respondents and rationalising the answers.

One part of the interpretation task is simply to report on the findings with an indication of the accuracy of the result. The other is to go one step further and state the implications of the results in terms of marketing decision making. This book will help the researcher judge the accuracy of his or her findings, but the wider interpretation of the results is dependent on having benchmarks from other surveys, experience in the sector and flair for deciding whether the cup is half full or half empty and what to do with the contents anyway.

SOME JARGON ASSOCIATED WITH DATA ANALYSIS

Most survey analysis packages emulate one of the first methods of automation used in data processing — the punched card. In the period just after the Second World War, a card with holes around the edge was used. Each card represented questions on a questionnaire and the surrounding holes were opened up at the edge by a punching machine to form a V in accordance with the answers. This meant that when all the cards were stacked together, a needle could be passed through the holes to pull out those that had not been punched and leave behind those that had. In this way the cards which were left behind could be quickly counted. Computers soon took over the reading of the punched cards and, during the 1980s, cards themselves were dropped to make way for the direct entry of numbers against the answers on the questionnaires.

The jargon which originated with the punched card is still used today for describing the method of coding up a questionnaire. Cards had 80 hole positions and these were known as *columns*. The term 'column' is in common use and refers to the list of numbers alongside the pre-coded answers. If a questionnaire requires more than 80 columns to cope with the responses, the researcher begins a new 'card' and, from that position in the questionnaire, the columns run once again from 1 to 80. In the example, the columns are identified by the number in brackets. What proportion of the products you buy are obtained from:

	Builders' merchants (12)	DIY shops (13)	Other distributors (14)	Direct from manufacturers (15)
0%	1	1	1	1
1–10%	2	2	2	2
11–40%	3	3	3	3
41–65%	4	4	4	4
66–99%	5	5	5	5
100%	6	6	6	6
DK[1]/ Refused	7	7	7	7

[1]Don't know

THE OUTPUT OF DATA

Even a survey with couple of hundred respondents can generate three inches of tabulations if each question is cross analysed by everything else. The result is daunting to the researcher whose aim is to reduce the data to arrive at a neat conclusion of what it all means and to decide the next steps to be taken.

The information required to write the report may come from many sources, perhaps survey data supported by some desk and qualitative research. The first task in coping with mountains of data is to evolve a report structure into which the information can be slotted. The logical order of the questionnaire will offer some guide to the structure of the report (see Figure 1.1) but need not be followed slavishly. Questions asked towards the end of the questionnaire may have been positioned there deliberately to suit the respondent who would be ready primed at that point.

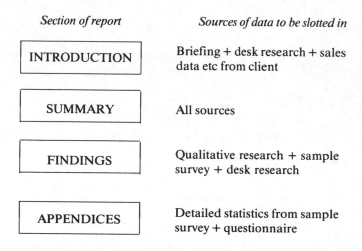

Section of report	*Sources of data to be slotted in*
INTRODUCTION	Briefing + desk research + sales data etc from client
SUMMARY	All sources
FINDINGS	Qualitative research + sample survey + desk research
APPENDICES	Detailed statistics from sample survey + questionnaire

Figure 1.1 Slotting survey information into a report format

Once the structure of a report has been laid out, the researcher's work is much easier. From now on it is a question of writing text and preparing summary tables to fit within the subheadings of the chapters. And this is the essence of data reduction and report writing — drawing out the key issues from the piles of data and relating it to the subject in question.

2

TYPES OF STATISTICAL DATA

■

CLASSIFICATION (OR NOMINAL) DATA

Much of marketing is about targeting certain types of consumer and market research helps identify these *segments* by collecting classification information from respondents. Classification data tends to be in a fairly standard form and covers age, sex, household composition, social grade, tenure of home etc. These data are used to cross analyse the key questions in the survey so allowing the researcher to compare and contrast the findings in different 'cells' of response. Typical classification questions are those which establish demographics, viz:

■ **Sex**
  — Male
  — Female

■ **Working status**
  — Working full-time/part-time
  — Not working
  — Retired
  — Student
  — Still at school

■ **Region of residence**
  — Scotland
  — Northern England
  — Midlands

— Wales and the West
— Southern England

These classification examples place individuals into groups with no gradation or distance between them and as such are referred to as *nominal* data. That is, the classification categories are not graded in size, getting bigger or smaller; they are simply different. Beyond these standard types of classifications, further nominal data could arise in a main survey. For example, a survey which sought political opinion or social attitudes may well also ask the following:

■ **Voting intention**
— Conservative
— Labour
— Liberal and Social Democrat
— Democrat
— Other party
— Will not vote

■ **Favourite daily newspaper**
— The Times
— Daily Telegraph
— Sun
— Mirror
— Daily Mail
— Daily Express
— Today
— The Independent
— Guardian
— Financial Times
— Star
— Other

Once again the individuals are grouped into classes which have no gradation one to the other and so they, too, are nominal data.

In such cases the researchers count the numbers of respondents falling in to each cell of the classification and arrive at a *frequency table*. Thus, for a survey of a 1000 adults, we might end up with data such as that shown in Table 2.1.

TABLE 2.1 ANALYSIS OF SAMPLE BY STANDARD REGION

Region of residence	Number interviewed (ie frequency)	(%)
Scotland	112	11.2
Northern England	300	30.0
Midland	210	21.0
Wales and the West	70	7.0
Southern England	308	30.8
Total	1000	100.0

Two points should be noted about the data in Table 2.1. First, the sum of the frequencies in the classification (ie the number of people interviewed) equals the sample size. In other words, each individual appears once and only once in response to a classification question which asked them where they lived. The second point is that each frequency has been expressed as a percentage of the total sample size. The percentages therefore add up to 100 per cent. It is percentages such as these that form the raw data of much survey analysis.

Underlying these data is a simple measuring system which scores the respondent as follows:

1 = Respondent falls into stated classification.
0 = Respondent does not fall into stated classification.

Data of this type are known as *binomial distribution data* and we shall return to them in a later section.

People interpreting the data are interested in quickly assimilating the *patterns* of response and these are markedly visible in the percentage distribution column. Thus, it is quite common in market research reports to show *only* the percentage column, though in such cases it would be expected to indicate the base or sample size either at the top or bottom of the table. In many tables it is also appropriate to round off the decimal points to eliminate any false sense of accuracy and to make the data easier to read. We have done this in Table 2.2.

TABLE 2.2 ANALYSIS OF SAMPLE BY STANDARD REGION

Region of residence	(%)
Scotland	11
Northern England	30
Midlands	21
Wales and the West	7
Southern England	31
Total	100
Sample size	*1000*

In this example people can only live in one area of the country and so the frequency table must add up to 100 per cent, ie 1000 respondents. However, there are many questions in market research where respondents can give more than one answer. Consider, for example, a question which asked motorists which monthly car magazines they read. Table 2.3 illustrates the possible results.

TABLE 2.3 READERSHIP OF POPULAR MOTORING MAGAZINES

Journal	Number interviewed	% Reading
Popular Motoring	991	50
The Motor	570	29
Cars Illustrated	545	27
Car Mechanics	332	17
Which Car?	310	16
Autosport	112	6
Other	572	29
Total sample size	*2000*	*

Respondents may read more than one journal and so column sums to more than 100%.

It will be noted that respondents may read more than one magazine and so could give more than one answer. As a result the calculated percentages in the right hand column far exceed 100 per cent. This is known as a *multi-response* question and it would be normal, in a market research report, to indicate that this is the case, for example as a footnote to the table.

RANKED (OR ORDINAL) DATA

We have just considered tables presenting data in the order recorded on the questionnaire. In some questions (including many classification questions) there is a natural order which it is important to maintain, irrespective of the result. These questions with natural orders, where there is an expressed precedence working from one end of the scale to the other, are known as *ordinal scales*. The numbers which establish the ranking (ie first, second, third etc) are known as *ordinal numbers*. Examples of ordinal scales are:

■ Respondent rating of effect of medicine:
   — Severe drowsiness
   — Moderate drowsiness
   — Little drowsiness
   — No drowsiness.

■ Product 'A' ranking compared with five other products tested:
   — 'A' ranked
   — First
   — Second
   — Third
   — Fourth
   — Fifth
   — Sixth.

■ Likelihood of buying the product over the next week:
   — Very likely
   — Quite likely
   — Neither likely nor unlikely
   — Not very likely
   — Not at all likely.

As before, the numerical data arise from frequency counts and percentages for each category.

It must be realised that the numbers sometimes used on ordinal scales (ie indicating the first, second, third etc preference) are not real numbers but are used only to indicate more or less of a preference for items being ranked. For example, if a respondent rates two products A and B on a scoring system of 'marks out of ten', then a score of six for product A and three for product B does not mean that A is liked twice as much as B. It only means that A is preferred to B. If A had been scored as eight and B as five (ie the same difference of three in the scores as above), it does not necessarily mean that A is liked more or less than it was with the person who had scored the products six and three.

When we think, or assume, that the distances between ordinal scale points *are* equal then 'marks out of ten' or 'marks out of five' form interval scales and we may wish to calculate average scores etc.

MEASURED DATA

In many questions respondents use real numbers in answer to survey questions. For example, men may be asked to state exactly (to the nearest pound) how much they spent on clothes last week. We have an option to leave the respondent free to suggest his expenditure on clothes but in practice it is unlikely they will be able to remember the exact figure. It is much easier if the question asks which band of prearranged expenditures would apply to them:

**£ spent last week for
those buying clothes**

1–10
11–20
21–30
31–40
41–50
●
●
●
●
200 or more

This grouping and its associated frequency counts is known as a *frequency distribution* and we shall return to it later. The numbers used here are real ratio numbers, ie if Peter spent £40 on clothes last week and Paul spent £20, then Peter spent twice as much as Paul. With such data we can perform all manner of statistical calculations and measure their validity.

There is one form of numbering scheme, popular with market researchers who use rating scales, which attaches an arbitrary set of numbers to the words of the rating scale. An example would be:

Verbal rating scale	Alternative scores	
	Descending rank	Weight around the centre point
Very good	5	+2
Good	4	+1
Neither good nor bad	3	0
Poor	2	−1
Very poor	1	−2

It must be understood that the numbers of such scoring systems are not ratio scale numbers (ie as with the example on clothing expenditure). Nor can one assume necessarily that they even form an interval scale. However, it must be said that the practice of assuming interval measurement is widespread in market research and researchers often calculate descriptive measures, such as averages, on them.

3

MEASURES OF LOCATION

∎

FREQUENCY DISTRIBUTIONS

We now turn to descriptive measures that can be calculated from the responses to survey questions. Much sense can be made of the numbers if tables showing frequency distributions are prepared. For example, if we have asked 1000 women how many fashion magazines they read last week, we would obtain 1000 numbers such as 2, 0, 4, 0, 1, 6, . . ., 0, 1 and so on. It is difficult to interpret 1000 individual numbers, so we form them into a frequency distribution (Table 3.1).

With this type of table it becomes more apparent how many people read fashion magazines and we can see that very few read more than one. But what we really require is a single number which is typical of the data values. Such single values are known as *measures of location* or *measures of central tendency*, commonly known as *averages*.

THE ARITHMETIC MEAN

The first of these measures considered is the *arithmetic mean*. Suppose we have data consisting of a series of measured numbers and that we have *n* (ie a certain number) of them. The measurements can be denoted symbolically by the labels:

$$x_1 \qquad x_2 \qquad x_3 \qquad x_4 \ldots x_n$$

where x_1 is the value (number) for the first respondent and x_n is the value for the last (*nth*) respondent. The arithmetic mean is denoted by the symbol (called 'x bar') and is written as $\bar{x}$.

$$\bar{x} = \frac{\Sigma x}{n}$$

TABLE 3.1 FREQUENCY DISTRIBUTION

Number of magazines read	Frequency (ie number of times mentioned)
0	237
1	588
2	97
3	30
4	15
5	12
6	9
7	7
8 or more	5
Total	1000

Now $\Sigma x = x_1 + x_2 + x_3 + x_4 \ldots x_n$ just means add up or sum and therefore Σx means add up the n measurements x_1, x_2 etc (n = the number of measurements being used). In other words, the arithmetic mean is obtained by adding up all the measurements and dividing by the total number of measurements.

As an illustration, lets us take a simple example of six children with ages ranging from 7 to 14 years (ie n = 6 measurements).

$$x_1 = 11, \ x_2 = 9, \ x_3 = 14, \ x_4 = 7, \ x_5 = 12, \ x_6 = 10$$

$$\bar{x} = \frac{11 + 9 + 14 + 7 + 12 + 10}{6} = \frac{63}{6} = 10.5 \text{ years}$$

It will be noted that the arithmetic mean lies somewhere in the middle of the six values.

Let us now suppose we want to calculate the average readership of women's magazines. In this case we asked each person interviewed how many magazines they read and we obtained discrete measurements (ie 0 magazines, 1 magazine, 2 magazines, 3 magazines, and so on). We had different numbers (technically speaking, frequencies) of women giving each value. Here a different formula has to be used to calculate the arithmetic mean from the frequency distribution:

$$\bar{x} = \frac{\sum fx}{\sum f}$$

where x = the value for each measurement (0, 1, 2, etc) and f = the frequency of occurrence of the value.

In words this formula says: take the value of x, multiply it by the number of times it was mentioned (f), total these figures and finally divide by the sum of the number of times mentioned (frequencies). It will be apparent that the sum of the frequencies (Σf) is equal to n, the total number of values.

As an example, let us return to the frequency of women's fashion magazine reading and calculate the average number (mean) read by people in the sample (Table 3.2).

TABLE 3.2 FINDING THE 'MEAN' READERSHIP OF WOMEN'S MAGAZINES

Number of magazines read (x)	Frequency (f)	fx
0	237	0
1	588	588
2	97	194
3	30	90
4	15	60
5	12	60
6	9	54
7	7	49
8 or more	5	40
Total	1000	1135

$$\bar{x} = \frac{\sum fx}{\sum f} = \frac{1135}{1000} = 1.135$$

We now have a useful statistic to bandy around. That is, we can say that the average (mean) number of women's fashion magazines read by people in the sample is just over one.

A further modification is a grouped frequency distribution and the example in Table 3.3 contains data on the amount spent on car servicing. Since we do not have a precise value for the amount spent on servicing (the response was collected as a ranged value) we take the midpoint of the range.

TABLE 3.3 FINDING THE MEAN FOR A GROUPED FREQUENCY DISTRIBUTION

Amount spent on car service (£)	Midpoint (x)	Frequency (f)
Up to 20	10	25
21–40	30	111
41–60	50	244
61–80	70	573
●	●	●
●	●	●
etc	etc	etc

The formula $\dfrac{\Sigma fx}{\Sigma f}$ is once again used but now x denotes the midpoint of the range values. The arithmetic means that have been calculated are single numerical figures which lie somewhere in the middle of the measurements being considered. They are said to be typical or representative of the measurements from which they have been calculated. They give quick comprehension of the data under review and provide benchmarks against which to make comparisons.

Another use for arithmetic means is for grossing up. For example, if we know the average wage of employees in a company and the total number of employees, then a simple multiplication will give the total wage bill. A drawback of the arithmetic mean is that it is greatly affected by one or more very untypical values. Two other kinds of averages, the *median* and the *mode*, attempt to overcome this problem of extreme values, and will be discussed shortly.

Before leaving the arithmetic mean it is worth mentioning a common occurrence in market research work. This is the rating scale to which numerical scores have been attached (see Table 3.4).

TABLE 3.4 TYPICAL RESULTS FROM A RATING QUESTION

Scale	Score (x)	Times mentioned (f)
Very important	5	20
Important	4	40
Neither	3	60
Unimportant	2	10
Very unimportant	1	10
Total		140

The arithmetic mean for the rating of importance can be calculated by the usual formula and is often referred to as the mean score in market research reports (Table 3.5).

Using the formula

$$\frac{\sum fx}{\sum f} = \frac{470}{140} = 3.4$$

gives the mean score.

TABLE 3.5 FINDING THE MEAN IN A RATING SCALE

Scale	Score (x)	Times mentioned (f)	fx
Very important	5	20	100
Important	4	40	160
Neither	3	60	180
Unimportant	2	10	20
Very unimportant	1	10	10
Total		140	470

THE MEDIAN

The median is the middle of a set of numbers, one half of which are larger and the other half smaller when all the measurements are arranged in order of magnitude. This alternative form of average overcomes a criticism of the arithmetic mean which is distortion through exceptional values.

Formally, if we have n measurements arranged in order, the median is the value of the $\frac{n+1}{2}$ th measurement. If n is an even number then there is no middle measurement as in the simple example below where $n = 6$.

20   21   22   23   24   25

The formula says take the $\frac{n+1}{2}$ $th = \frac{7}{2} = 3.5th$. Thus, we take the mid-point between the 3rd and 4th measurements and the median value is 22.5.

THE MODE

A further way of obtaining an average which is not affected by extreme or untypical values is to use an average called the mode. This is defined as the measurement or value which occurs most often. For example, Table 3.6 shows the ages of 30 children arranged in a frequency distribution.

TABLE 3.6 FREQUENCY DISTRIBUTION/AGES OF 30 CHILDREN

Age (x)	Number of children (f)
7	6
8	15
9	4
10	3
11	2
Total	30

The age which occurs most often, and is therefore the mode, is eight years. More children are that age than any other in the distribution.

The mode is useful for discrete frequency distributions. A frequent use of the mode is where a frequency distribution of shoe sizes can tell a shoe manufacturer which are the most popular sizes of shoes to make. In our fashion magazine example, the three measures of central location are all very similar, viz:

Arithmetic mean = 1.135
Median   = 1
Mode   = 1

4

MEASURES OF VARIABILITY (DISPERSION)

◾

USING HISTOGRAMS TO SHOW THE DEGREE OF CLUSTERING

The measures of central location or central tendency we have been considering are valuable pieces of information which summarise the data under review, but they do not tell the full facts about data. Whereas an average shows where most of the measurements are clustered, it does not tell us how clustered or how dispersed are the individual measurements around the average. If we are told that the average height of Welshmen is the same as the average height for Scotsmen, we might be tempted to think that height frequency distributions were the same. However, by drawing histograms of the two height distributions it might be apparent that one shows heights clustered around the average (Scotsmen), while the other (Welshmen) reveals a much wider spread of heights either side of the average (see Figure 4.1).

STANDARD DEVIATION AND OTHER MEASURES OF MEASURE OF DISPERSION

Single numerical values can be calculated from data to show the

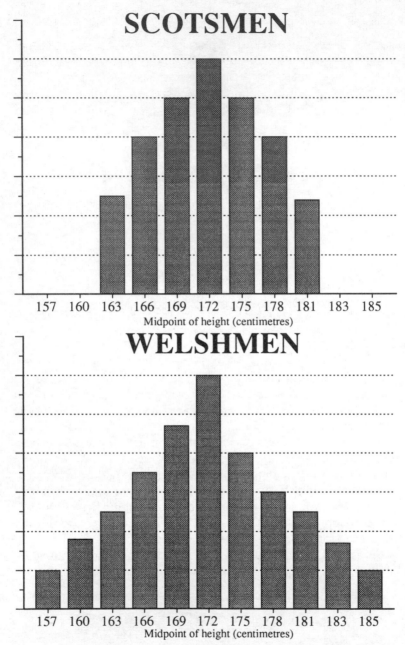

Figure 4.1 Histograms of height frequency distributions

dispersion of data measurements around their average. These values are known as measures of variability or measures of dispersion, the simplest of which is called the *range*. This is defined as the largest measurement in the data minus the smallest measurement. It is therefore a very simple calculation.

Range *per se* is not a very satisfactory measure as it is based on only two of the original measurements, and therefore can be considerably different if the highest and lowest measurements are untypical or extreme values.

The most important measures of variability are the *variance* and the square root of the variance: the *standard deviation*. They do not have the merit of simplicity of calculation as does the range, but they are widely used in statistical analysis, as they have a number of advantages.

For a set of measurements the formula for calculating the variance and the standard deviation are:

$$Variance = V = \frac{\sum (x - \bar{x})^2}{n}$$

$$Standard\ deviation\ = \sqrt{V} = s = \sqrt{\frac{\sum (x - \bar{x})^2}{n}}$$

Using a previous data set on the ages of six children (n = 6 values) with an arithmetic mean of $\bar{x} = 10.5$ years we have.

Age of children (x)	$x - \bar{x}$	$(x - \bar{x})^2$
11	0.5	0.25
9	−1.5	2.25
14	3.5	12.25
7	−3.5	12.25
12	1.5	2.25
10	−0.5	0.25
$\Sigma = $ 63	0	29.50

$$Variance = V = \frac{29.50}{6} = 4.917$$

$$Standard\ deviation = \sqrt{V} = \sqrt{4.917} = 2.217\ years$$

The standard deviation (or the variance) measures how closely the ages of the children are grouped around their mean measurement. The more concentrated are the measurements around the mean, the smaller is the standard deviation. The more the spread of the measurements about their mean, the larger the standard deviation.

The standard deviation, which is probably more often used than the variance, is not so affected by extreme or untypical measurements as is the range. It plays an important role in showing the precision of, say, an arithmetic mean resulting from a random sample.

When data have been grouped into a frequency distribution a modified formula has to be used to calculate first the variance, and eventually the standard deviation.

$$V = \frac{\sum f(x - \bar{x})^2}{\sum f} \qquad SD = s = \sqrt{\frac{\sum f(x - \bar{x})^2}{\sum f}}$$

When two frequency distributions have the same arithmetic mean, the variability of these two distributions may be compared by calculating their respective standard deviations. The one with the higher standard deviation will be more variable. When the two arithmetic means of the frequency distributions are different, a measure of relative dispersion is needed. This is called the *coefficient of variation* and is defined as:

$$CV = \frac{standard\ deviation \times 100}{arithmetic\ mean}.$$

Returning for a moment to the measurement of people's height, if we find that there is a considerable variation in our required measurements, the coefficient of variation provides the answer. Using the coefficient of variation we can see that a standard deviation of 5 inches indicates relatively greater variability if the mean height is 60 inches than if it is 72 inches.

$$CV = \frac{5 \times 100}{60} = 83.3\% \qquad CV = \frac{5 \times 100}{72} = 69.4\%$$

The first group, with a mean height of 60 inches, is relatively more variable in height than the second group.

One vexed question has to be posed at this stage. What is the correct divisor to be used in the formula for the variance (standard deviation)? Is it n (as has been presented here) or is it $n - 1$, as given in some statistical textbooks? With small sample sizes, say less than $n = 50$, when estimating a population variance from the sample data, then it is appropriate to use $n - 1$ as the estimate using n tends to underestimate the population variance. With large samples it makes little difference which is used.

THE BINOMIAL DISTRIBUTION

When respondents in a survey give an answer which slots into just one single category (ie is not multi-response) then the data follow the binomial distribution. An example would be buyer/non-buyer of a product; another would be social class ABC1/C2DE. If we score, for example, buyer = 1 and non-buyer = 0 then if we have n_1 buyers and n_2 non-buyers ($n_1 + n_2 = n$, the total sample size) the arithmetic mean is given by:

x	f	fx	
1	n_1	n_1	
0	n_2	0	
	n	n_1	$= \Sigma fx$

$$\bar{x} = \frac{\Sigma fx}{\Sigma f} = \frac{n_1}{n} = proportion\ of\ buyers = p$$

Similarly, it can be shown that the variance is given by $p(1 - p)$ and the standard deviation by:

$$\sqrt{p(1-p)}$$

Equivalent terms of expressing the proportion as a percentage ($p\%$) are $p\%$ ($100 - p\%$) and

$$\sqrt{p\% \, (100 - p\%)}$$

Much market research data are expressed as percentages and therefore these are important formulae that we shall be using later.

5

SAMPLING DISTRIBUTIONS AND STANDARD ERRORS

■

NORMAL DISTRIBUTION

When a sufficiently large sample is selected from a population (say over 100) the resulting averages or percentages, if plotted on a graph, will assume the shape of a bell-shaped curve known as *normal distribution* (see Figure 5.1). The distribution of the results

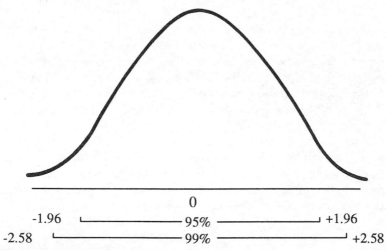

Figure 5.1 Distribution of sample means

in this way is fundamental in helping us make inferences from sample surveys.

The normal distribution is particularly important to us in market research as it tells us that a known proportion of values lie beyond certain multiples of the standard error (more on this in a moment). Some typical examples are: 95 per cent of values are within the range of population average ± 1.96 standard errors, only 5 per cent of values are outside this range; 99 per cent of values are within the range of population average ± 2.58 standard errors, only 1 per cent of values are outside this range. This property of the normal distribution is useful when we come to learn how to make inferences about the population average and when we can draw only one sample from that population.

At this point it is instructive to introduce the idea of *probability*. When it is stated above that only 5 per cent of values are outside a range, we are saying that there is a chance, or probability, of 1 in 20 (ie 5 per cent) of the items or people that we sample will fall outside the stated range. We will return to probability ideas when discussing confidence intervals.

CALCULATING THE SAMPLE ERROR

So far we have introduced the above concepts in terms of drawing many samples from a given population; in practice we only draw one sample. How, then, do we know the value of the standard error which has been derived from repeated sampling of the population? Luckily, there is no need to draw from a large number of different samples to estimate it; it can be estimated from the single sample we normally select.

If we select a sample n (greater than 100) and obtain a numerical measurement from each person — for example their personal weekly income in £ — we can calculate the standard deviation of the actual sample values, as detailed above. The standard error of the arithmetic mean of the sample is then given by:

$$Standard\ error\ (\bar{x}) = \frac{s}{\sqrt{n}}$$

In other words, the standard error is obtained by dividing the sample standard deviation by the square root of the sample size (n).

EXAMPLE

A sample of $n = 200$ men in the UK report their weekly beer consumption and the following results are obtained:

$$Mean = \bar{x} = 5.6 \text{ pints per week}$$
$$Standard \text{ } deviation = 2.1 \text{ pints}$$
$$Sample \text{ } size = 200$$
$$\therefore Standard \text{ } error \text{ } (\bar{x}) = \frac{2.1}{\sqrt{200}} = 0.148 \text{ pints}$$

What is the practical use of the standard error? As we shall see later, it is a key statistic for assessing the precision of an arithmetic mean calculated from a sample.

When the sample survey data are in the form of binomial data, such as the respondent fitting the category of buyer/non-buyer, then the arithmetic mean of the sample is the proportion (percentage) of the sample who are buyers. The standard error of this percentage is given by:

$$Standard \text{ } error \text{ } (p\%) = \sqrt{\frac{p\% \text{ } (100 - p\%)}{n}}$$

EXAMPLE

A random sample of $n = 400$ in an opinion poll yields the result that $p = 40\%$ are pleased with the Government's performance.

$$n = 400$$
$$p\% = 40\%$$
$$100 - p\% = 60\%$$
$$Standard \text{ } error \text{ } (p\%) = \sqrt{\frac{40 \times 60}{400}} = \sqrt{6} = 2.45\%$$

We will use this result later to assess the precision of the sample survey percentage ($p\% = 40\%$).

CONFIDENCE INTERVALS

How can we make use of these calculated standard errors and the normal distribution theory? They can be used to calculate confidence intervals or confidence limits (as they are sometimes called) to determine the precision of the arithmetic mean (or percentage) from the single sample we have selected.

For large samples (n greater than 100) the sampling distribution of the means will follow the normal distribution and we can use certain properties of that distribution. In drawing random samples from a population with a mean of $\bar{x}$ then, as we have said previously:

1. 95 per cent of the samples will have means falling in the ranges $\bar{x} \pm 1.96$ standard errors of the mean;
2. 99 per cent of the samples will have means falling in the range $\bar{x} \pm 2.58$ standard errors of the mean.

Now we can turn this argument round, and say that the true mean ($\bar{x}$) of the population will have a 95 per cent chance (probability) of falling in the range:

Sample mean ± 1.96 (Standard errors of the mean)

$$ie \; \bar{x} \pm 1.96 \left[\frac{s}{\sqrt{n}} \right]$$

This range is known as a *95 per cent confidence interval*. A 99 per cent confidence interval will be given by:

$$\bar{x} \pm 2.58 \left[\frac{s}{\sqrt{n}} \right]$$

EXAMPLE

The previous data on men's beer consumption were as follows:

$$Mean = \bar{x} = 5.6 \; pints$$
$$Standard \; deviation = s = 2.1 \; pints$$
$$Sample \; size = n = 200$$
$$Standard \; error \, (\bar{x}) = \frac{s}{\sqrt{n}} = 0.148 \; pints$$

A 95% confidence interval for the mean $\bar{x} = 5.6$ pints is given by:

5.6 ± 1.96 (0.148)
5.6 ± 0.29
ie from 5.31 pints to 5.89 pints.

What is the interpretation of this 95 per cent confidence interval? We have conducted a sample survey to estimate $\bar{x}$, the average beer consumption for the whole population of men in the UK. Because we have only taken a relatively small sample, the average produced by the sample ($\bar{x} = 5.6$) is not a fixed quantity since it is subject to sampling variability. What we are saying is that although we do not know what the population value $\bar{x}$ is, we are 95 per cent confident that it would lie within the band of 5.31 pints to 5.89 pints in 19 out of 20 sample surveys we might carry out. There is obviously a 1 in 20 chance that we are making an incorrect statement when we derive the 95 per cent confidence limits, but this is the risk which must be taken when carrying out sample surveys. The level of risk can be reduced by setting 99 per cent confidence limits and therefore having only a 1 per cent chance of being wrong. As explained earlier, setting a higher sample size can also improve the precision of the confidence interval.

EXAMPLE ON % DATA

Using the opinion poll data cited above, we have:

$$n = 400 \ sample \ size$$
$$p\% = 40\%$$
$$Standard \ error \ (p\%) = 2.45 \ \%$$

95% confidence interval for p% = 40% is given by:

$$40\% \pm 1.96 \ (2.45\%)$$
$$40\% \pm 4.8\%$$
$$ie \ 35.2\% - 44.8\%$$

Note how wide the confidence limits are for such a small sample size.

THE EFFECT OF SAMPLE SIZE ON STATISTICAL PRECISION

The biggest revelation to most people learning about sampling is that for most intents and purposes they can forget about the size of the universe they are researching. What matters is the *absolute size* of the sample.

Let us concentrate for the moment on the influence which sample size has on the precision of the result. Say, for example, we wanted to find out how many people in Birmingham bought butter last week. We do not need to know the population of the city or agonise over whether we need a 5 per cent sample, a 10 per cent sample, or whatever — that is totally irrelevant. All we have to do is to choose a sample which is *big enough to give us a result which will be acceptable for our purposes.* As long as the sample is selected randomly, 2000 interviews with food shoppers would give us results which are precise to ± 2.2 per cent at 95 per cent confidence limits. And 2000 people, as it happens, represent only 0.2 per cent of households in the city. To reinforce this point, we could carry out a random survey of 2000 people throughout the whole of the UK and ask them about their butter purchases and the result would still have the same level of precision (ie ± 2.2 per cent at the 95 per cent confidence limits). And, just for the record, 2000 people represent less than 0.01 per cent of the number of households in the UK.

So the sample size (n) plays a vital role in determining the precision of sample survey results. It is an integral part of the standard error formulae and therefore it determines the width of the confidence intervals. To be precise, it is not the sample size itself which is important, but rather the square root of the sample size. Thus, if we wish to double the precision of our sample survey estimates (ie make the confidence interval width one half of what it currently is), we do not have to double the sample size, we have to make it four times as big! Think about the cost implications of this. If an interview costs £20 per head and the chosen sample size is $n = 2000$, then the total survey cost is very high. Assume that the survey result obtained is that 50 per cent of people smoke cigarettes. Then the 95 per cent confidence interval is calculated in the normal way and we have the following summary:

Sample size	Survey statistic	95% confidence interval	Total survey cost
2000	50%	± 2.2%	£40 000

Increasing the sample size from 2000 to 8000 has a predictable effect on precision and cost:

Sample size	Survey statistic	95% confidence interval	Total survey cost
8000	50%	± 1.1%	£160 000

The survey has probably become prohibitively expensive for what is a non-practical reduction in precision. The confidence limits of ± 2.2 per cent are likely to be good enough for practical purposes and it is probably better to carry out three further surveys on different topics, for one's money, than spend it on improving the precision of one survey from ± 2 to ± 1 per cent.

A further important point is that it is not the overall sample size that is always the criterion. Quite often it is the size of sub-samples which have to be fixed at a certain size. For example, let us examine some holiday data with a sample of 200 people selected randomly amongst four age bands (Table 5.1). This as a 'dipstick' survey as the accuracy of the results from the total sample would only be ±7 per cent (at the 95 per cent confidence level). However, whether we like it or not, cost and time often result in such small samples.

TABLE 5.I WHETHER HOLIDAY TAKEN OUTSIDE COUNTRY IN LAST YEAR: BY AGE

Holiday taken	Total %	Age			
		Under 25 %	26–35 %	36–55 %	Over 55 %
Yes	27	45	30	24	13
No	73	55	70	76	87
Total	100	100	100	100	100
Sample size	200	50	50	50	50

In this example it appears that among the whole population, just over a quarter have had a holiday abroad and that there is some relationship between age and holidaying abroad. However, the level of sampling error for the age group sub-samples is higher than for the sample as a whole and possibly the differences which are shown merely reflect this. The reason the sampling error for the sub-samples will be greater is that they each include only 50 respondents compared with 200 for the sample as a whole.

A problem often found in market research is that sample size is selected on the basis of the precision sought from the whole sample. At the analysis stage the data may show differences between groups of respondents and yet the size of the sub-samples is too small to allow any statistical confidence to be attached to the differences. If comparing the sub-samples is important (and it usually is) then the size of the overall sample will have to be decided with this in mind. In practice nearly all market researchers carry out surveys on samples of just a few hundred and the most they can do is comment on the shift in patterns between the sub-groups which perhaps is indicative of a trend. At the very least, if the data is technically unreliable in this way, the problem should be acknowledged in the report text. This applies particularly if the information is going to be used for a major decision.

In the UK tourism survey, we might have to assume before the study begins what proportion may take their holiday abroad. Assuming that 25 per cent is the penetration of that group and we wish to get confidence limits of ± 2 per cent approximately, then we will require that sub-sample base to be 2000. As they are just one of four cells of the population we are sampling, this means that the total sample size must be about 8000 — a far cry from the 200 sample that was carried out.

DETERMINING SAMPLE SIZE FOR A GIVEN PRECISION

Before a sample survey is carried out, the client often states that he requires a survey data to be of a stated precision. For example, he may wish a sample survey arithmetic mean, which may be the $\bar{x} = 5.6$ pints per week in the previous beer example, to be precise to ± half a pint and have 95 per cent confidence in this prediction. What size of sample does he need to ensure such precision and what formula is used to calculate the correct sample size?

Let $\pm d = $ the required confidence interval
$z = $ the normal distribution constant to give a specific per cent confidence level
$s = $ standard deviation
$n = $ required sample size

In the beer example:

$$\pm d = \pm \tfrac{1}{2} \text{ pint}$$
$$z = 1.96 \text{ for 95 per cent confidence limits}$$
$$s = 2.1 \text{ pints}$$

The formula for sample size n is:

$$n = \frac{z^2 s^2}{d^2}$$
$$\therefore n = \frac{(1.96)^2 (2.1)^2}{(0.5)^2}$$
$$n = 68$$

For binomial percentage data:

Let $\pm d =$ the required confidence interval
$z =$ the normal distribution constant to give a specific per cent confidence level
$p\% =$ estimate of percentage being measured
$n =$ required sample size

For the opinion poll data, let us set the desired 95 per cent confidence interval to be $\pm$ 1 per cent on a result we expect from the survey which will be that 40 per cent will have a certain voting intention. That is p (per cent) = 40 per cent. Therefore:

$$\pm d\% = \pm 1\%$$
$$z = 1.96$$
$$p\% = 40\%$$

The formula for n is:

$$n = \frac{z^2 p\%(100 - p\%)}{d^2}$$

$\therefore n = 9220$ people of voting age

SIGNIFICANCE TESTING

Often we wish to compare two statistics from one survey or two statistics from separate surveys. An example of the former case would be to compare the statistic 'percentage of men who smoke' with the statistic 'percentage of women who smoke'. The second case may be comparing the 'percentage of men who smoke' survey this year with the 'percentage of men who smoke' from last year's survey.

Obviously both statistics, being based on sample surveys, are subject to sampling variability. Imagine two annual surveys of 2000 adults which give the following results:

Year	% men who smoke
1987	34.3
1988	35.7

Has smoking among men increased? We know from our confidence intervals that both results have sampling errors of about ± two per cent. The difference (35.7% − 34.3% = 1.4%) is less than the sampling error and therefore may not indicate a real change. Could not the truth in both years be that the level of smoking among men is constant at 35 per cent? It is not unreasonable with the 1987 sample of 2000 to get a survey result of 34.3 per cent that in truth is 35 per cent. Similarly we may argue that the 1988 result of 35.7 per cent is also not unreasonable, even though the real proportion may be 35 per cent.

What we need is a method for determining how large differences in survey results have to be before we can confidently report them as real differences.

Significance testing is the statistical method for deciding objectively whether a difference is real or can be explained by sampling variation. When the observed difference between the two percentages is greater than a certain margin, then we say that the difference is statistically significant and we can conclude that a real change in the level of smoking has taken place.

It is not possible in this short exposition of statistics in market research to give a full description of the theory of significance testing. What will be given now is an example of one of the most popular significance tests used in market research.

TEST OF TWO INDEPENDENT PERCENTAGES

This is the case cited above where we wish to assess whether two percentages obtained from two different sub-samples (eg age 16/24; age 25 and over) are really different. Alternatively we may be comparing results from two different survey samples.

Just as single survey percentages have a measure of sampling variability (the *standard error*), so does the difference between two percentages. The standard error of the difference between two percentages p_1 and p_2 is given by:

$$Standard\ error\ (p_1 - p_2) = \sqrt{pq\left[\frac{1}{n_1} + \frac{1}{n_2}\right]}$$

where n_1 and n_2 are the respective sample sizes, and where

$$p = \frac{n_1 p_1 + n_2 p_2}{n_1 + n_2}$$
$$q = 100 - p$$

A significance test is carried out by comparing the actual difference $(p_1 - p_2)$ with its standard error. We calculate the criterion:

$$z = \frac{p_1 - p_2}{Standard\ error\ (p_1 - p_2)}$$

and if z is equal or greater than 1.96 we say that the difference is significant at the 5 per cent level. We conclude that the observed difference is greater than would be expected if the two samples were drawn from populations where the two percentages were actually equal. This is the hypothesis being tested — is there really a difference between the two percentages or could their difference be explained by sampling variability? The interpretation of the 5 per cent significance level is that there is a 1 in 20 chance that we make an incorrect decision when we conclude that the two sample percentages are exhibiting a real difference.

The following example shows the use of this significance test in a practical example. Samples of n_1 = 900 motorists in Scotland and n_2 = 1600 motorists in England yield p_1 = 43 per cent and p_2 = 40 per cent respectively, who drove more than 15 000 miles in the last 12 months. The significance test is used to ascertain whether this sample difference of $p_1 - p_2$ = 3 per cent is a real difference among all motorists in these two countries.

$$p = \frac{(900 \times 43\%) + (1600 \times 40\%)}{900 + 1600} = 41.1\%$$

$$q = 100 - \text{p} = 58.9\%$$

$$Standard\ error\ (p_1 - p_2) = \sqrt{(41.1\%)\,(58.9\%)\left[\frac{1}{900} + \frac{1}{1600}\right]} = 2.05\%$$

$$z = \frac{p_1 - p_2}{Standard\ error\ (p_1 - p_2)} \qquad = \frac{43 - 40}{2.05} = 1.46$$

The value of the z criterion is less than the critical value of 1.96 needed for the 5 per cent significance level and the conclusion is that we *cannot* state that the proportion of long distance motorists is different for the two countries — that is, there is no significant difference in the two proportions.

In this example, a significance level of 5 per cent was used as we wished to limit the possibility of an incorrect decision to 1 in 20 (ie 5 per cent). If we wished to be more cautious and only accept a 1 per cent error level then the critical value of z would be 2.58. The 5 per cent and 1 per cent levels of significance are those most commonly used in market research. The critical values 1.96 and 2.58 are those values mentioned earlier and are related to the normal distribution.

6

SAMPLING THEORY

∎

THE SCIENCE OF FINDING OUT A LOT FROM A LITTLE

The topic of sampling is an essential one for market researchers since almost all market research is conducted using samples. It is therefore important that researchers understand the main concepts of sampling and are familiar with the sampling methods available to them. The aim of this chapter is to acquaint researchers with the main principles of sampling and with the sorts of sample designs that are used in practice. Our concentration will be in the first instance on *random* samples because all tests of accuracy depend on each and every member of the population having an equal chance of selection. Later on we describe non-random samples and show how here the principles are quite different.*

The first question to be asked is 'Why do we wish to draw samples from a defined population instead of carrying out our research among *all* members of that population?' In other words, should we carry out a census rather than use a sample. Clearly in our research we are trying to find out certain things about the whole

---

* Itinerant sampling specialists and those wanting to know about the underlying statistical and mathematical theory are referred to *Sampling Techniques* by W G Cochran (3rd edn, John Wiley, Chichester, 1977) and *Survey Sampling* by L Kish (John Wiley, Chichester, 1965).

population and it therefore makes sense to do so with as complete accuracy as possible. This is one point in favour of a census. However, that method of obtaining survey results has a number of drawbacks. First, the populations from which we select our samples are usually very large, consisting of many thousands or even millions of people. Thus to carry out a survey on all of them would clearly take a very long time — one thing that market researchers do not have, being required usually to produce results very speedily.

Secondly, censuses cost an enormous amount of money. Therefore it seems that recourse must be made to using samples to carry out market research studies. In practice this is what always happens and the properly selected sample has a great part to play in research. A sample is selected from a population to give representative and unbiased data about that population. All the methods of sampling described below aim to have this property, namely that the survey results obtained from the sample are broadly the same as those that would have been obtained had the whole population been surveyed.

The use of the word 'broadly' in this context needs explaining. It would not be expected that a sample, no matter how carefully selected, would estimate exactly a population value (eg the percentage who smoke), but what is required from any sample design is that if it were repeated a large number of times, it would reflect, *on average*, the same result as a whole population census, giving estimates without bias. This is what is meant by the term 'representative sample'.

A fundamental point of sampling is that the selection of people to interview must reflect the population values accurately most of the time. It is not much use getting the right result on average if repeating the sample design gives very widely scattered results around that average. A good sample design will give the client the true result most of the time with only small margins of error. These margins (known as sampling errors) can be calculated for the sample designs used in market research, as we have already seen. Their magnitude depends on two factors: the size of the sample and the sample design. Thus in market research the aim of drawing samples is to make inferences about survey populations and to do so with acceptable margins of error. Fortunately for us this is easily possible and over the years many thousands of sample surveys have been carried out in the fields of commercial and social research, where the sample designs have produced acceptable results.

POPULATION DEFINITION

The fundamental question when selecting a sample is 'what is the definition of the population from which sample is to be selected?' In any sample survey, the results refer to the defined *population* and to none other. The use of the word population in the sampling context is different from its everyday use which is the number of people who live in the UK or any other nation. In sampling, the population (sometimes called the universe) is the aggregate of items (eg people, smokers, addresses) from which the sample is to be drawn.

It is essential that the population is rigorously defined before the sample design is contemplated and that this definition is agreed by the researcher and client. For example, it may be decided to carry out a survey among 'motorists in this country'. This is far too vague a description of the population and it needs further definition. What does the phrase 'in this country' mean? Does it refer to England, Great Britain or the UK? If this understanding is not made crystal clear, the researcher could be embarrassed by covering too little or too much territory in the survey. The second word which needs tightening up is 'motorist'. In a survey on buying petrol, the definition of a motorist may be anyone who drives a car at any time, whereas for a survey concerned with car repairs and servicing it could be defined as car owners only.

In this section we demonstrate how samples can give accurate information about a population most of the time. We also show how, by increasing the size of the sample, it is possible to obtain a more precise estimate of what is happening within the population. The approach used here was originally given by Stuart.*

---

* *Basic Ideas of Scientific Sampling*, Stuart, (2nd edn, Griffin, 1976).

WORKING OUT THE AVERAGE FOR A POPULATION FROM A SAMPLE

Consider a population of $n = 6$ students who have been given marks out of twenty for an English examination. The six marks for students labelled A to F are shown below:

A	B	C	D	E	F
1	5	7	9	9	11

The population average (arithmetic mean) mark is $\bar{x} = 7$ and it is this population result that is to be estimated by means of sampling. Of course, in practice the population average is unknown and in order to find out what it is, the sample survey is carried out. In this case, as it is known, it is possible to see how well an unbiased and biased sampling plan can perform and what the effect of increasing the sample size will be.

Consider drawing a sample of $n = 2$ students from the population of $n = 6$ and forming their average mark as an estimate of the population average $\bar{x} = 7$. It would be possible to do this a number of times with such a small population and with such a small sample size. In fact it does not take long actually to draw all possible 15 samples of size $n = 2$. In fact there are $\frac{t\,(t-1)}{2}$ pairs from t objects. This has been laid out in full in Table 6.1 opposite and the population average has been estimated from each sample average.

It can be seen that the sampling plan only gives an exact estimate of the population average for just two of the 15 samples. It should also be noted that for some of the samples the estimate produced is very far from the population average (eg 3 and 10). However, there is a broad tendency for the sample average to be clustered around the value of seven, with sometimes an overestimate and sometimes an underestimate. The remarkable fact about the 15 samples as a group is that if the average is taken of all the 15 population estimates from the samples, then this will be found to equal seven, the population average.

Thus the sampling design which takes all possible samples of $n = 2$ from this population is what is known as an *unbiased*

TABLE 6.I SAMPLING PLAN FOR DETERMINING THE AVERAGE MARKS OF STUDENTS

Sample of students		Marks		Sample average
A	B	1	5	3
A	C	1	7	4
A	D	1	9	5
A	E	1	9	5
A	F	1	11	6
B	C	5	7	6
B	D	5	9	7
B	E	5	9	7
B	F	5	11	8
C	D	7	9	8
C	E	7	9	8
C	F	7	11	9
D	E	9	9	9
D	F	9	11	10
E	F	9	11	10

sampling plan. That is, if it is repeated a number of times, it will give estimates which on average and in the long run will correctly estimate the population value. Clearly when using this sampling plan an estimate will sometimes be produced that is considerably different from the population average, as was the case for the first sample of students A and B. This is the penalty one must pay when using a sample instead of a census, although the problem of less accurate samples can be overcome by increasing the sample size.

TABLE 6.2 SAMPLE SIZES

Sample average	Frequency of occurrence
3	1
4	1
5	2
6	2
7	2
8	3
9	2
10	2
Total	15

At this point we can refer back to some technical terms which we discussed in Chapter 3. If the above 15 sample averages are formed into a *frequency distribution*, then this distribution is

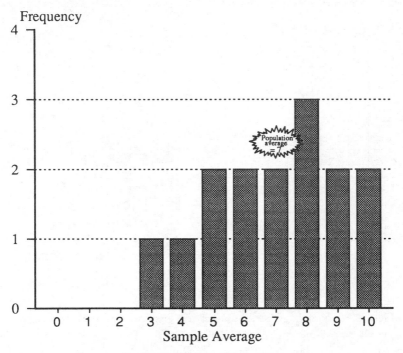

Figure 6.1 Sampling distribution of the arithmetic mean

known as the *sampling distribution* of the *arithmetic mean*. It can be shown diagramatically as in Figure 6.1.

Just as it is possible to calculate the average of this distribution, so it is possible to calculate its standard deviation (see Chapter 4 for details). When dealing with a sampling distribution, the standard deviation is given a special name, the *standard error of the mean*. This is to distinguish it from the usual calculation of the standard deviation from the data values of a *single* sample of respondents. The standard error is an important concept when explaining sample precision and the calculation of sampling errors. Here it is seen to be a measure of spread or concentration of the sample averages around the population average, arising from applying the sampling plan a number of times.

Freqency

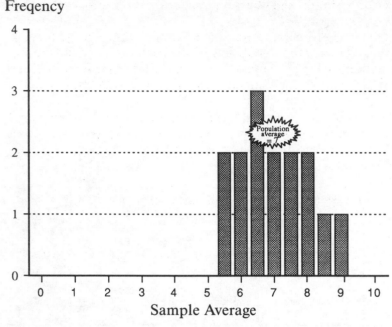

Figure 6.2 Sampling distribution of the arithmetic mean — increased sample size

Now what is the effect on the sampling distribution and the standard error of increasing the sample size? Consider all possible samples of $n = 4$ from the sample population of $N = 6$ students; there are again 15 of them and if you wished to confirm this you could write them down in tabular form as in the earlier example. The distribution of their arithmetic means may be shown pictorially (Figure 6.2).

It is visually apparent and can be checked by calculation, that the average of this sampling distribution is equal to seven, the unknown population average. The sampling plan is therefore unbiased. More important is the fact that whereas with samples of $n = 2$ the sample averages ranged from 3 to 10, they now, with $n = 4$, only range from 5.5 to 9. In other words the sampling plan with a larger sample size produces estimates which are more closely grouped around the population average. Thus, the standard error is lower and the sampling plan produces more precise results.

This is a general result and is of wide applicability. It means that the larger the samples taken, the more precisely can the population values be estimated by the sample. As shown in Figure 6.2, the shape of the sampling distribution is becoming smoother and more regular about the population average. Eventually, as the sample size gets very large (say, greater than 100), the sampling distribution takes on a special shape and becomes a well-known statistical distribution, the *normal distribution*, with helpful properties. (See also Chapter 5.)

TABLE 6.3 BIASED SAMPLING METHOD

Sample of students		Marks		Sample average
A	B	1	5	3
A	C	1	7	4
A	D	1	9	5
A	E	1	9	5
B	C	5	7	6
B	D	5	9	7
B	E	5	9	7
C	D	7	9	8
C	E	7	9	8
D	E	9	9	9

A further point to demonstrate at this stage is that of a biased sampling method. Suppose that in our population of $N = 6$ students that student F was for some reason a non-respondent. Thus, the samples of $n = 2$ will not be able to include that student. There are therefore only ten possible samples of $n = 2$ that can be selected (Table 6.3).

The average of these ten sample averages is equal to 6.2, which does not equal the population mean value of seven. The sampling plan is therefore *biased* as it does not in the long run produce the correct population result on average.

7

RANDOM SAMPLING

■

RANDOM (OR PROBABILITY) SAMPLING

The word random in statistics has a precise meaning — it does not imply haphazard. In a random sample, every member of the population has a known (but not necessarily equal) probability or chance of selection. For this reason it is sometimes known as probability sampling. The sample is drawn by some chance process such that the person drawing the sample has no say as to which members of the population appear in the sample. Random sampling can be distinguished from other methods of sampling used in market research and described below, where the sample selector (normally the interviewer) decides which members of the population appear in the sample.

METHODS OF RANDOM SAMPLING

SIMPLE RANDOM SAMPLING

This is sometimes known as unrestricted random sampling and is a method of selecting n items from a population of N items such that every item in the population has an *equal* chance of selection in contrast to more complex random designs, where groups of units are selected at a first stage and then sub-sampled at a second stage.

With small populations the sampling method may be achieved

by numbering the population members from 1 to N and then drawing n random numbers between 1 and N from published sets of tables of random numbers. An extract from such a set is shown in Table 7.1. Suppose a sample of $n = 10$ is required from a population of $N = 100$. First number the population members from 00 to 99. Pairs of random digits are then selected from a random start point in the table and these form the numbers for the ten selected population members. Thus, in the table the marked up numbers show that population members 95, 73, 10 etc form the sample of $n = 10$. If a number is thrown up more than once (eg this occurred with population member 76 in the table) the selection would move on to another number.

In practice this sampling method is not very often used by itself, but is used in conjunction with other, more efficient methods of sampling. Readers may wish to use the table to carry out their own sampling distribution simulations of, say, random samples of $n = 5$ and $n = 10$ from the population of $N = 100$ as outlined in the previous section.

SYSTEMATIC RANDOM SAMPLING

When the population size is large, random number selection becomes tedious and we may use a simpler method known as *systematic random sampling*. It is not necessary to number all the population members from 1 to N, but simply to know the value of N, the population size, and have available a list of the population members.

To select a systematic sample of n items, first calculate the sampling interval defined as:

$$k = \frac{\text{Size of population}}{\text{Size of sample required}} = \frac{N}{n}$$

Then take a random number between 1 and k as the starting point for first member of the sample. By counting through the subsequent members of the population and selecting every kth member after the random start and doing this $n - 1$ times determines the remaining $n - 1$ members of the sample.

TABLE 7.I RANDOM NUMBERS

22	35	85	15	13	60	11	14	10	**95**	45	07	31	66	49
09	98	42	99	64	24	51	79	89	**73**	53	94	13	38	47
54	87	66	47	54	88	97	54	14	**10**	35	80	39	94	88
58	37	78	80	70	88	26	49	81	**76**	16	04	61	67	87
87	59	36	22	41	23	83	01	30	**30**	90	89	00	76	33
68	34	30	13	70	84	26	34	91	**64**	70	29	17	12	13
74	57	25	65	76	83	92	12	06	**76**	56	62	18	37	35
27	42	37	86	53	44	39	52	38	**79**	99	49	57	22	77
00	39	68	29	61	99	66	02	79	**54**	16	08	15	04	72
29	94	98	94	24	08	02	73	43	**28**	31	16	93	32	43
67	19	01	71	74	60	76	21	29	**68**	12	41	94	96	36
02	94	37	34	02	47	70	90	30	86	96	93	02	18	29
79	78	45	04	91	16	92	53	56	16	10	47	48	45	88
87	75	66	81	41	40	01	74	91	62	35	81	33	03	76
34	86	82	53	91	00	52	43	48	85	45	37	59	03	09

Suppose a sample of $n = 10$ is to be selected from a population of $N = 1000$. The sampling interval is calculated as $k = \dfrac{1000}{10} = 100$ and the random number between 1 and k turns out to be 41. Therefore counting down the list of 1000 population members on the list and selecting every 100th person after person 41 identifies the remaining 9 sample members as:

141	241	341	441	541	641	741	841	941

The resulting sample will be seen to cover all parts of the population list and this is a point where the systematic sample scores over the simple random sample, especially if the population list is in a special order (see below). There is no reason why, in theory, a simple random sample should not give sample members from just the first 100 population members. It is possible, although unlikely, in practice. When the population members are in random order this should not matter and then the two sampling methods will give the same results in the long term.

Systematic sampling is especially useful in market research when sampling from directories, professional body lists of members, etc. The only serious drawback to the method is when the list is in order of values of some key variable (eg a list of building society members in order of amount invested). In such cases a systematic sample, depending on the random start, will sometimes give a biased sample. When the random start is at the lower end of the sampling interval, the resulting sample will have a lower average amount invested than will a sample based on a random start near the top of the sampling interval.

STRATIFIED RANDOM SAMPLING

When drawing from certain populations it is often the case that the sampler knows something about the population which may be used to improve the sample design. In the previously cited population of $N = 100$ used for demonstrating a simple random sample, the following population members were selected for the sample using the table of random numbers:

95   73   10   76   30   64   79   54   28   68

Now suppose that the first 50 members (00–49) listed in the population were men and the last 50 members (50–99) were known to be women. The principle of stratification says that this information, if known, should be used. Consider the simple random sample selected which ends up with three men and seven women. There is nothing wrong with this as, in the long run, samples of 10 will on average give the correct balance of five men and five women. What is done in stratified random sampling is to divide the population up into known groups, called *strata*, then select a simple random sample from each *stratum*. Thus, in the present example, a simple random sample of five men would be selected from the men's stratum (members 00–49) and a separate simple random sample of five women from the womens' stratum (members 50–99). Protection is thus given from any imbalance that may arise from a single simple random sample.

Stratification gives a much better random sample than does simple random sampling when the variable or characteristics in which strata are formed is correlated with the variable being measured by the sample. For example, if the variable being estimated by the sample is the percentage of people who smoke, then if 60 per cent of men smoke and 40 per cent of women smoke (50 per cent overall), the above simple random sample of three men and seven women would give a very distorted estimate of the overall smoking level. If on the other hand, the level of smoking is 50 per cent for both men and women, this particular simple random sample will be no worse than a stratified sample. When the variable being measured by the survey sample is not the same for the different strata, then the stratified sample will produce population estimates with far less sampling errors than will the simple random sample.

In the above example of stratified sampling, an identical sampling fraction was taken in each stratum, ie a sample of 1 in 10 was selected from the men's stratum and the same fraction from the women's stratum. This is known as *stratified sampling* with *proportional allocation* and is the most popular variant of the technique.

Sometimes it is desired to use different sampling fractions in the various strata. This is known as *disproportional allocation* and is usually done in market research to obtain a minimum sub-sample size in each stratum. An example here would be a sample in England and Wales, where every one of the nine standard regions had to have at least a sub-sample size of 300 in a total sample size of 2700. Because of their very different sizes, a pro-portionate sample would give some regions only a sub-sample size of about 100, which could be thought of as being too small for accurate separate regional analysis.

A further occasion when disproportionate sampling is used in survey work is when sampling population with members that vary greatly in size (eg businesses). If the aim of the survey is to estimate the annual turnover of the market in £m, then 'number of employees' may be used as a basis for forming strata. In indus-trial markets the larger firms account for the bulk of the total turnover, a phenomenon very often referred to as the 80 : 20 rule because the distribution of companies by size results in 80 per cent of the purchases (or sales or whatever) being accounted for by 20 per cent of the companies. For this reason it is argued that it is more important for the sample to contain a much larger pro-portion of large firms than medium or small firms. The sampling fractions are then chosen using a statistical theory known as *optimum allocation*, which gives the lowest sampling errors for a fixed survey cost. Typical sampling fractions in such an example might be as follows:

Small firms	1 in 20
Medium firms	1 in 10
Large firms	1 in 2

MULTI-STAGE SAMPLING

Quite often the population falls into natural groupings. In the population of electors in Great Britain, for instance, the electors live in polling districts. A number of these polling districts form wards and a number of wards in turn group together into a con-stituency or local authority area. If a sample of $n = 600$ electors is required, it is possible to select a stratified random sample using, say, regional and urban/rural stratification. This would give a widely scattered sample of $n = 600$ respondents, one from each of the 600 separate constituencies. This, however, is rather an expensive and time-consuming way of getting 600 interviews since, if only 60 interviewers were used, they would have to travel widely to get their assignment of ten interviews.

Multi-stage sampling is a way of getting over this problem and helps to reduce survey costs. At the first stage a random sample of constituencies (known as primary sampling units or PSUs) is selected. At a second stage a random sample of one or more wards is selected from each of the *selected* constituencies. Other stages may be added as required until suitable economic interviewing areas are obtained. In the example quoted, a suitable design would be to have 60 polling districts, situated in 60 wards of 60 selected constituencies, with each interviewer carrying out ten interviews.

The advantage of multi-stage sampling, apart from economy, is that stratification may be used at each stage of the sample selection. The main drawback is that such samples have increased sampling errors over single stage stratified samples and measure population variables less precisely. The increased error comes from the sampling errors incurred by each stage of sampling.

SAMPLING WITH PROBABILITY PROPORTIONAL TO SIZE (PPS)

Quite often the first-stage or primary sampling units may vary considerably in size. For instance, if we take constituencies as primary sampling units (PSUs), it is known that they will contain different numbers of electors. When the sampling units vary in size it is not good practice to use simple random sampling in their selection. To do so would mean that a constituency with 80,000 electors would have the same chance of appearing in the sample as a constituency with only 40,000 electors. This imbalance can be corrected by taking a *fixed* sampling fraction from each constituency and ending up with a variable number of interviews in each area. The problems created for field-workers can be overcome by sampling PPS. In this method each constituency would be given a chance of selection which is proportional to its number of electors. An illustration of the mechanics of the method is given in Table 7.2.

TABLE 7.2

Constituency	Number of electors	Cumulative number of electors
1	20 000	20 000
2	40 000	60 000
3	10 000	70 000
4	60 000	130 000
5	60 000	190 000
6	20 000	210 000
7	20 000	230 000
8	10 000	240 000
9	80 000	320 000
10	80 000	400 000
Total	400 000	

Suppose it is required to select a sample of *four* constituencies from a population of *ten* constituencies with probability proportional to the number of electors. The procedure is as follows:

1. Cumulate a running total of number of electors (third column);
2. Determine the sampling interval required which is:

$$\frac{\text{Total number of electors overall}}{\text{No of constituencies within sample}} = \frac{400\,000}{4} = 100\,000$$

3. Choose a random number between 1 and 100 000, say 50 000 which will be used as a starting point;
4. Look in the cumulative total electors column and see where this 50 000th elector lies. He lies in constituency number two and this constituency is the first one chosen in our sample;
5. Add on the sampling total interval successively to the random start three times to identify the other three selected constituencies in the sample. They will be:

50 000 + 100 000 = 150 000	Constituency 5
150 000 + 100 000 = 250 000	Constituency 9
250 000 + 100 000 = 350 000	Constituency 10

Note how this approach has resulted in there being a greater number of larger rather than smaller constituencies in the sample.

The main advantage of sampling PPS at the first stage is that if an *equal number* of interviews are carried out in each selected primary sampling unit, then the overall chance of selection for each population member will automatically be equal.

SEMI-RANDOM SAMPLING (RANDOM WALK)

The random sampling methods described above are ones in which the interviewer has no say in the selected procedure. Interviews must be achieved only with the people generated by the sampling scheme and no others. There is also another form of sampling used in market research which attempts to 'mimic' a random sample. Commonly referred to as 'random walk', it is also known as 'random route' or 'point and route' sampling.

The principle is that the interviewer is given a random address at which to conduct the first interview and thereafter a set of rules are followed in order to locate the other addresses. The interviewer continues to interview at every nth address in the street, alternatively turning left and right into other streets whenever they are encountered. Special instructions are given on how to deal with non-private dwellings, cul de sacs, blocks of flats and open spaces. The method is not a pure random sample as much depends on the detail of the instructions given to the interviewer and her bias in carrying them out.

When the starting addresses are selected they are usually part of a normal multi-stage stratified random sample and therefore the resulting sample of addresses can be very similar to a pure random sample as described above. The method is best suited to sampling in urban areas, for example, for samples of housewives. It can be used in rural areas, although here interviewers are given more than one random starting address in case they run out of subsequent addresses on their walk.

Random walk sampling should be used with call-backs for those addresses where no one is at home when the interviewer first calls. When fully applied, therefore, it is not a cost-effective method. It is useful when there is no time to draw a full random sample from the electoral register. Some researchers do not use call-backs but set overriding quota controls (see the section on quota sampling) for working/non-working people to balance what would be a biased sample of households obtained during the day. The prime advantage it has over non-random sampling techniques is that it requires interviewers to interview in defined areas where they might not necessarily choose to go if allowed latitude. It can therefore give a much better sample than a quota sample.

8

SAMPLING FRAMES

THE QUALITIES OF A SAMPLING FRAME

A sampling frame is a list of all the N members of a population from which the sample may be conveniently selected. One of the first questions to be asked when a random sample is being considered is, 'is there a suitable sampling frame for the population being sampled?' It makes the sampling process so much simpler if there is a good list of population members. Such a list should have the following properties:

1. It should contain a list of members of the defined population (or at least those members who are in the defined population should be identifiable). An example would be a list of the members of an accountancy professional institute with the names of retired members indicated (this could then be used as a sampling frame of working accountants).
2. The frame should be a complete, up-to-date list of the population.
3. No population member should be listed more than once. This would almost certainly occur, for instance, in lists built up of plumbers chosen from *Yellow Pages* as some plumbers will pay for entries in directories outside their home area and will be named more than once.
4. The list should contain information about each individual that could be used for stratifying the sample.

It is fair to say that most lists used in practice do not fully meet all these requirements.

Researchers in the UK have access to three main sampling frames when drawing samples of the general population of domestic establishments and private individuals — the electoral register, telephone directories, and the postal address file (PAF). The most used frame is the electoral register with the PAF becoming more popular for sampling addresses.

THE ELECTORAL REGISTER

The electoral register is published on 16 February every year, using data supplied by individual householders in the UK relating to the previous 10 October. It gives the names and addresses of all persons aged 18 and over and also those who are due to become 18 during the life of the current register. It remains in force until 15 February of the next year. Each constituency produces a register that is available in a number of booklets, one for each polling district. These can be grouped into wards, local authority areas, etc for use in multi-stage sampling. In urban areas the register is arranged alphabetically by street name and within street name by house number. At each house the electors are usually listed alphabetically by surname and then by first name within surname. In very rural areas, however, the names of electors are arranged alphabetically. Clearly the register is out-of-date by four months when it is published and gets progressively more out-of-date during its life. Some people will have died and others will have moved home (12 per cent of people in any one year) and new houses will have been built. For this reason it is obviously a better sampling frame for addresses than for individuals.

From what has been said above, it is apparent that the register is an adequate but not perfect sampling frame. It is often used to select samples of addresses or individuals. One essential point in its favour is that it is available in a number of ways. It can be inspected locally at town halls and libraries and it can be used for sampling at the British Museum or the Government Social Survey, where a full national set is kept. Finally, one may buy copies of the individual constituency registers from electoral registration offices at town halls.

SAMPLING INDIVIDUALS FROM THE ELECTORAL REGISTER

The convenient way in which the register is arranged makes it easy to draw samples of electors. Usually systematic random samples of electors are taken from wards or polling districts with varying degrees of clustering. Thus, a random number is chosen which identifies an elector and every nth elector is selected. However, most surveys require more than just a sample of electors and often a sample of adults aged 15 and over is needed.

To supplement the sample of electors the following procedure (formulated by Kish)* is often used to obtain the non-electors and those who have moved house. The interviewer at each selected elector's household makes a list of all persons aged 15 and over who are not on the electoral register and numbers them from one to n, alphabetically by surname and initials. The interviewer then selects one of these listed people for interviewing using a Kish selection grid, an example of which is shown in Table 8.1.

If the interviewer was at the fourth elector's household and there were three listed persons not on the register, then the selection grid shows that in this case the first listed person would be interviewed. At the fifth house the interviewer finds out there are three people aged over 15 and these are listed alphabetically. In this household the Kish grid would instruct that interviewer to interview the second person on the list for that household.

It will be noted that wherever there are three persons listed,

---

* **Kish grid/box** A table for use by interviewers in random sample surveys, to select one person from a household. The procedure gives an approximately equal chance of selection to each member of the household. It is sometimes used as an alternative to the birthday rule in order to select a non-elector for interviews in addition to interviewing the named elector. Source: *Dictionary of Market Research*, Market Research Society (MRS) and Incorporated Society of British Advertisers (ISBA).

TABLE 8.I KISH SELECTION GRID

Address serial number	\multicolumn{6}{c}{Number of listed persons}
	1	2	3	4	5	6 or more
1	1	2	1	4	3	5
2	1	1	2	1	4	6
3	1	2	3	2	5	1
4	1	1	1	3	1	2
5	1	2	2	4	2	3
6	1	1	3	1	3	4
7	1	2	1	2	4	5
8	1	1	2	3	5	6
9	1	2	3	4	1	1

one-third of the time it is the first who is interviewed, one-third of the time it is the second and one-third of the time it is the third person, and so on.

Most sample designs ensure that overall electors are selected with equal probability, but this is not true for these additional 'non-electors'. They are selected with varying probabilities that depend on the number of names on the electoral register at their household and the number of 'non-electors' from whom they are selected. They each, therefore, have to be given the following weight in the analysis of the survey results:

$$\frac{\textit{number of non-electors within household}}{\textit{number of names on register for that household}}$$

The above sampling scheme for individuals will sometimes result in two interviews in one household. This is objectionable for some studies where the client has good reason for insisting on only one interview per household for, say, a population of people aged 14 and over. An efficient procedure here is to select a sample of electors from the register in the usual way, but not necessarily to carry out an interview with that selected person. The interviewer goes to the *household* of the selected elector and forms a list of people aged 14 and over (as for non-electors) and uses the Kish grid to select one of them. At the time of analysis each selected person is given a weight to correct for unequal selection probabilities. The weight is defined as:

$$\frac{\textit{number of persons aged 14+ within household}}{\textit{number of names on register for that household}}$$

This gives not too great a range of weights for the selected respondents. If households had been selected with equal probability and then a single person selected, the range of weights would be the numbers of qualifying people in each household, mostly ranging from one to five. Such extreme weighting increases sampling errors and an inefficient sample design will result.

In addition to drawing samples of people it is often necessary to draw a random sample of men and women from the register. This is done by examining every nth name on, for example, the polling district register and only including it in the sample if it is a name with the required sex. Alternatively, one may select every nth man's/women's name, but this takes slightly longer for the sampling clerks to carry out. Whichever method is used there is still the problem of distinguishing between men's and women's names.

SAMPLING ADDRESSES AND HOUSEHOLDS FROM THE ELECTORAL REGISTER

Because of the way the register is laid out it is possible to draw random samples of addresses (households), usually samples of housewives or heads of households. This can be done in two ways:

1. By taking every *n*th address from the register using the street address as a guide. The addresses are listed conveniently in street order.
2. By the method of 'firsting', where a sample of electors is drawn but the selected elector's address is only included in the sample if he is the first *named* elector at that address. This gives a self-weighting sample removing the imbalance of selection probability caused by addresses having different number of electors. Both methods give problems in rural areas where electors are listed alphabetically. The sampling clerk has to inspect the whole polling district register to see whether any selected elector is the first named at his address.

As most addresses contain only one household, the resulting sample of addresses is almost a sample of households: to convert it to a household sample one just includes in the sample *all* households at each address. In practice, however, it is normal to have an upper limit of three households per address.

THE POST OFFICE POSTCODE FILE

All addresses now have a postcode and a premises code and therefore each address can be uniquely defined in the post office sampling frame. It can therefore be used to draw random samples of addresses and is becoming increasingly popular for this purpose. Because of the layout of the postcodes, going from a postcode district down through to sector codes and then to postcodes, it is convenient for drawing multi-stage samples. Another advantage is that it is available in various forms including a computer file, from which it is easy to draw systematic random samples.

A number of commercial organisations such as CACI and Pinpoint offer sampling services using the electoral register and the postal address file (PAF). They can supply multi-stage stratified random samples of electors or addresses. For a set of sampling areas, they can also give quotas of people to be selected (see also Chapter 9).

BUSINESS-TO-BUSINESS SAMPLING FRAMES

It is often a surprise to market researchers to learn that there is no single listing of all industrial/business-to-business establishments in the UK. There are no government sources to which we can turn for comprehensive lists. The Business Statistics Office publishes a list called the *UK Directory of Manufacturing Businesses* which is available from HMSO. The lists contain companies making returns to the *Business Monitor*, the official statistical organ for publishing industrial output and sales. There are six parts to the series and each covers three major industries which in turn are broken down into minimum list headings of the Standard Industrial Classification. However, companies making returns to *Business Monitor* have to elect to be in the list and in the event it is only a minority that does so. The list is, therefore, not comprehensive by any means, nor does it provide telephone numbers.

In the absence of any official lists, the business-to-business market researcher turns to one of the many commercial directories available. Specific trades and industries may have their own excellent lists compiled by a trade association, thus there are good lists of food manufacturers, plumbers and consulting engineers from yearbooks or trade association sources. If the researcher is seeking a general list of industry, one of the compendiums of industrial establishments such as *Kompass*, Dun & Bradstreet or *Yellow Pages* will prove most useful.

KOMPASS

Kompass is one of the best directories for industrial sampling. It has a fairly comprehensive listing of industrial establishments of more than 25 employees and each company is classified by the products it makes, the number of employees and a turnover band.

The directory comes in four volumes. The first lists the products and services offered by the 40,000 companies and is used by researchers to build up a frame of who does what. The second volume covers the same number of companies but this time it features company information such as details on size in numbers of employees and turnover. The third volume contains financial information on 30,000 companies and the fourth volume lists 100,000 companies showing their parents and subsidiaries.

Most usefully *Kompass* can be accessed 'on-line' from a computer terminal which allows the researcher to select samples by keying in instructions on product codes (or industry types), region and company size. Since *Kompass*' on-line database is swelled by the inclusion of some other directories such as *Kellys* and *Dial Industry*, it is much larger than the hard copy, numbering over 150,000 companies.

DUN & BRADSTREET

The Key British Enterprises directory provides profiles on the top 20,000 firms in the UK. Each entry gives financial data on turnover and capital, details of the company's trade, trade names and trading styles and a full list of directors by name and function. A section of the directory breaks the listing of companies into standard industrial classifications (SICs) and geographical groupings. A detailed summary of the financial performance is given, together with share structure and the board of directors.

As with *Kompass, Dun & Bradstreet* listings are available on-line and researchers can select by SIC and region. Also like *Kompass*, the on-line database is much larger than the hard copy and contains nearly 350,000 firms.

YELLOW PAGES

A common misconception about *Yellow Pages* is that it is a listing of companies which have paid for an entry. This is not the case. It is the most comprehensive listing of all businesses in the UK as every business on the phone (and which aren't?) has an automatic free entry under the trade classification of its choice. A business could, of course, pay for an expanded or display entry, either in its 'home' directory or one further afield and this could lead to the duplication of names across the books.

However, *Yellow Pages*, through its 'Business Database', will sort and sift the 1.7 million business-to-business establishments (including retailers, colleges and not-for-profit organisations along with manufacturers and merchants). From this large listing it can provide a special de-duplicated list of businesses in any of its trade headings for a relatively modest sum per 1000 companies requested. *Yellow Pages*' Business Database also has the ability to stratify by size and geographical location of company and this is an important requirement for business-to-business samples.

9

QUOTA SAMPLING

ABOUT QUOTA SAMPLES

As with random sampling, quota samples are used to estimate certain facts about a defined population. However, unlike random samples where every member of the population has a known chance of selection, quota samples are based on the deliberate selection of groups of people so that the aggregate picture reflects the total population.

METHOD OF SELECTING QUOTA SAMPLES

Quota samples are selected in the following way. The researcher chooses certain characteristics by which to set quotas, which suppose that some relevant data is known about the population for those characteristics. The interviewers are then instructed to select set numbers (or quotas) of respondents with those characteristics. The simplest method is to use independent quota controls, illustrated in the Table 9.1 which is for an interviewer's quota of 40 interviews.

If each interviewer is given these numbers of interviews to carry out, then the total sample will consist of 50 per cent in each age grouping. The quota numbers are set such that a known population age split is obtained. Also, balance is obtained in this example for sex and social class. As long as the interviewer fills

TABLE 9.1 NON-INTERLOCKING QUOTA CONTROL

Sex	Number of interviews	Age	Number of interviews	Social grade	Number of interviews
Male	19	Age under 35	20	ABC1 class	17
Female	21	Age 35 and over	20	C2DE class	23
Total	40		40		40

the separate cells of the quota, she is at liberty to interview any-one she wishes. Thus, we may end up with all 19 males under the age of 35 — clearly not a balanced sample. To overcome this problem we can set interlocked quota controls (see Table 9.2).

TABLE 9.2 INTERLOCKING QUOTA CONTROLS

Age	Social grade	Sex male	female	Total	Grand total
Under 35	ABC1	4	3	7	20
	C2DE	7	6	13	
35 and over	ABC1	4	6	10	20
	C2DE	4	6	10	
Total		19	21	40	40

Now the 19 males are spread into age and class categories according to known population data, and a more representative sample is obtained. It is usual practice to mix quota controls, interlocking some characteristics and leaving others independent (Table 9.3).

TABLE 9.3 INTERLOCKING QUOTA CONTROLS

Age	Male	Female	Total	Social grade	Total
Under 35	11	9	20	ABC1	17
35 and over	8	12	20	C2DE	23
Total	19	21	40		40

It is important to realise that the sample design for national quota samples often follows that for random samples right up until the final respondent selection stage, where it differs. Primary sampling units are usually selected using a stratified, multi-stage, PPS sample. The final geographical area defined for carrying out the quota selection may vary from a whole town down to a single polling district or a few streets only. The choice will be dictated by such things as speed and availability of local quota setting information.

CHOICE OF QUOTA VARIABLES

The quota variables which are chosen for a sample depend on:

■ the availability of data for a large number of different geographic areas;

■ up-to-date data;

■ interviewers being able to classify people correctly on the quota variables, eg social class;

■ the quota controls should be correlated with the response variables being measured by the survey. For example, a study among housewives for 'convenience foods' should always have a working/non-working quota control as usage of such products could easily be different for working housewives.

Traditionally, quota samples of adults in the UK use age, sex, social class and working status as controls. Usually some particularly pertinent quota control is set for a survey, an example being a heavy/medium/light user quota for a product. In addition, some overriding general instructions are usually given about carrying out some of the interviewing in the evening and at weekends. A point to note here is that interviewers rarely interview in the street, as is popularly assumed, but usually interview people at home.

ADVANTAGES AND DISADVANTAGES OF QUOTA SAMPLING

The principal advantages of quota samples are their relatively low cost — up to half that of a random sample of a similar size. Secondly, they have the advantage of speed, giving survey results much more quickly than random samples, the latter requiring selection processes from sampling frames and time-consuming call-backs on the not-at-homes.

The main drawbacks are those associated with bias and sampling errors. As the selection of respondents is controlled virtually exclusively by the interviewers, the quota sample always runs the risk of obtaining a biased sample of the population, for instance, people who are more available for interview. This can create distortion if survey issues are unrelated to or irrelevant to not being at home very often. Furthermore, there is no probability mechanism involved in quota sampling and so it is not possible, except in special ways, to calculate sampling errors. (There is conflicting evidence on this subject with one camp suggesting that quota samples have the same levels of sampling errors as random samples and another claiming that they have twice their sampling error!)

On balance we tend to believe that if quota sampling is carried out correctly, it is a very suitable, lower cost alternative to random sampling.

Quota samples are often used where survey results are not required to fine degrees of accuracy, eg product tests for preference, and where little or no bias is expected. They are also very useful for minority sampling. Some of the bias in a particular quota sample may be removed by weighting. For example, suppose we have set an age, sex and social class quota of adults and we find the resulting sample is biased in terms of working/not working. If we know the correct distribution for working status then we can weight the sample to return it to the correct levels.

WHERE TO GET QUOTA-SETTING DATA

In the UK, the Office of Population Censuses and Surveys regularly publishes data on a national and regional basis for such variables as sex, age and marital status. In the years following the decennial census they supply data for more variables and split it down to very small areas. Obviously these data soon become out of date.

Most large market research firms carry out large-scale random surveys on a regular basis and some publish volumes of statistics for the setting of quotas. Some of them also run omnibus surveys in which one single question may be asked (along with others from similar clients). If the question is, for example, relating to the ownership of a motorcycle then analysis by sex, age and social class of those responding 'yes' will give quota-setting information for the population of motorcyclists.

If time is not available for collecting the quota-setting data in this way, then as a last resort, one may wish to use the method of *contact quota sampling*. Here, one sets a national quota sample of adults using, for example, age, sex, class and working status controls. Interviewers fill this quota control and whenever they come across someone who fits the quota control *and* owns a motorcycle, they complete an additional questionnaire on motorcycling, while other respondents in the quota simply complete a short demographic questionnaire. Clearly there are serious cost implications in such levels of screening to find people appropriate to interview.

RANDOM LOCATION SAMPLING

In this method, for each sampling point, a few streets are chosen with probability proportional to size (PPS) to the number of electors. Interviewers have to quota sample in these streets using a simple age, sex and working status quota. No social class quota is given (nor would it be feasible in such a small area), but a large number of sampling points ensures a good social class spread. Even so, if in the first analysis of results there is seen to be bias on social class, the sample can be weighted.

USE OF QUOTA SAMPLES

It has been roughly estimated that 60 to 70 per cent of market research is conducted using quota samples. Clearly, if the method was consistently giving badly biased samples and misleading conclusions, it would soon be discredited. It is a fact that general election forecasts using surveys based on quota samples are no less accurate than their random counterparts. Also, for a wide range of consumer goods, brand share data match well for surveys collected using both sampling methodologies.

10

TYPICAL MARKET RESEARCH SAMPLE DESIGNS

∎

When designing a national sample design for a study it is necessary to take into account most of the techniques and ideas put forward in the previous chapters. In this chapter we describe typical and well-known market research sample designs.

A STRATIFIED RANDOM SAMPLE FOR A READERSHIP SURVEY

This survey example is used to estimate readership levels for newspapers and magazines and the universe is defined as adults aged 15 and over in Great Britain. A two-stage stratified random sample is used and is selected as follows:

1. Wards are taken as first-stage sampling units and they are formed into 40 main strata by interlocking non-overlapping portions of ITV areas, metropolitan/non-metropolitan counties and Registrar General's planning regions.
2. Within the main stratum, wards are grouped into areas with more or less than 10 per cent of evening newspaper coverage.
3. Within each resulting substratum, wards are ordered by the

percentage Labour vote at the most recent local government election.

A total of 1512 wards are thus selected with probability proportional to the most up-to-date electorate figures. Within each ward, a polling district is then chosen with probability proportional to the most up-to-date electorate.

The electoral register is used as a sampling frame and within each polling district a systematic random sample of electors is drawn. To supplement this sample of electors a sample of non-electors is taken, not using a Kish grid, but a recently developed method (the Marchant-Blyth method)* for obtaining a self-weighting sample. The price to pay for a self-weighting sample is that on rare occasions two non-electors as well as one elector are sampled at an address.

Interviewers call and recall on the selected respondent and, as in all random surveys, are not allowed to accept substitutes. Obtaining a high response rate is essential for the randomness of the sample to be preserved and in this survey a response rate of about 70 per cent is usually obtained.

A TYPICAL NATIONAL QUOTA SAMPLE FOR AN ATTITUDE SURVEY AMONGST HOUSEWIVES

This survey example measures attitudes to coffee among housewives in Great Britain. Although it is not quota survey, the sampling points are selected in the same way as for a random sample. All constituencies in Great Britain were stratified in the following way:

1. By Registrar General regions.
2. By four urban/rural groups within each region.
3. By an index of socio-economic status derived from census constituency results.

---

* A full description of the method is given in the *Journal of the Market Research Society* 1973, vol 15, pp 157–62.

One hundred and eighty constituencies were selected at random with probability proportional to electorate size. Within each constituency, interviewers were asked to select 12 housewives according to quotas. These consisted of an interlocking age and social class quota and an independent quota on working status.

■

FORECASTING

■

TYPES OF FORECAST

The purpose of forecasting is to allow management to plan ahead. Without a view of the future, opportunities could be missed or investment made with no chance of a financial return. Four different types of forecast are relevant to the market researcher.

ECONOMIC FORECASTS

These paint a broad picture of the environment in which a company will be operating. They include a prediction of gross domestic product (GDP),* inflation, unemployment, balance of payments, plus a number of other parameters such as money supply, consumer spending, public sector borrowing and so on. The market researcher is interested in economic forecasts for the effect they have on the markets his company supplies, ie they are a backcloth. The market researcher would be unlikely to become involved in the preparation of economic forecasts as this is a specialised activity of econometricians. In any case, there is little need to do so as the financial press regularly publishes economic forecasts from specialist forecasting organisations (eg National

---

* GDP is the value of all the output of goods and services produced by a country's economy in a period — usually a year.

Institute of Economic and Social Research), the treasury and the merchant banks.

ENVIRONMENTAL FORECASTS

The economic forecast covers the financial environment in which a company operates. There is, however, a wider environment which encompasses the social, political and legal scenes. The relevance of wider issues will differ according to the business of the company. All companies are affected by major wars and the depletion of basic resources such as oil, gas and coal. Others will be affected, to a greater or lesser extent, by changes in fashion, climate, social attitudes, politics and specific legislation. Environmental forecasts are generally prepared by social scientists and published as long-term predictions.

MARKET AND PRODUCT FORECASTS

These are fundamental to the market researcher as they are concerned with specific sectors. The term is generally applied to forecasts of the end-user markets into which products are sold and forecasts for the product itself. The forecast of end-user demand is an important input in the product forecast.

SALES FORECASTS

These are a combination of what will happen to a company's sales as a result of the market environment and what will happen if the company introduces a new level of sales and promotional effort. It is, therefore, partly a statement of intent (a target) and partly a true forecast.

All forecasts must have a horizon, be it weeks or years. Conventionally, researchers use three important breaks:

■   Short-term forecasts concerned with periods up to a year;

■   Medium-term forecasts which look beyond a year as far as three years;

■ Long-term forecasts which are predictions beyond three years.

The time periods attributed to short, medium and long-term forecasting are entirely arbitrary and have changed over the last few decades. In the late 1960s and early 1970s economies and markets had greater stability and company forecasts stretched to five years. The shock waves created by the Yom Kippur War of 1973 have shortened the medium term to two to three years; longer than this would be beyond the realms of reasonable accuracy. Even these periods are changeable within the specific context of companies and their markets. In the fast-moving world of computers, long-term may be one to two years whereas a manufacturer of chemicals operates in an industry with a predictable ten year cycle, so long-term predictions could be pushed out to ten years and still maintain acceptable levels of accuracy.

THE ROLE OF FORECASTS INSIDE A COMPANY

Market and sales forecasting play a role in a number of areas of company planning.

CORPORATE PLANNING

The forecasts of the economic environment and the market enable the corporate planners to steer the future course of the company. They highlight general opportunities and, just as important, pinpoint the blind alleys and areas of decline.

PRODUCT AND MARKET PLANNING

The product and market plans are used to set company objectives and establish budgets for promotion and selling which are needed to achieve goals. Product and market forecasts are action orientated. It is from these that companies plan their entry into new markets, or their withdrawal from those offering limited opportunities. The more detailed the forecast, the more precise the action can be. A forecast of regional growth prospects allows a company to concentrate its efforts where they will pay greatest dividends. Forecasts for sub-groups of products similarly allow detailed planning for each sector.

SALES PLANNING

The sales plan is based on the forecast of sales which the company believes it can achieve. The sales forecast cannot be viewed in isolation; it represents a share of the total market which can realistically be attained and this, in turn, depends on the strengths and weaknesses of every competing supplier and the level of resources each commits in support of its own sales.

PRODUCTION PLANNING

Once agreed and accepted the sales plan becomes the master document on which all other internal company plans depend. The first of these is the production plan which is designed to ensure that productive resources are available to manufacture the product mix. Careful production planning is necessary to ensure good deliveries and productive efficiencies. The production manager may face the difficult choice of whether to produce large quantities in bulk, store them and live with expensive financing and warehousing costs, or to remain flexible, manufacturing to meet orders but paying the penalty of lost economies of scale.

FINANCIAL PLANNING

The production schedule will incur costs, the most important of which are stocks, tooling, machinery and plant. The sales and marketing plan will require money to be spent on promotion, selling, delivery and clerical processing of orders. The sales forecast affects the flow of cash into the company and if the predicted cash flow cannot be reconciled with predicted costs in the months ahead, loan options must be agreed with banks well in advance to ensure the lowest possible interest charges. Thus the financial plan is drawn up using the sales and production budgets and adding to them the overhead burden necessary to run the business.

SELECTING THE FORECASTING METHOD

Forecasts attempt to predict the future, therefore it is necessary that the forecast is expressed in appropriate values and in time periods which are conducive to the exercise. Values should ideally be inflation free, such as numbers of products, tonnes or gallons. Monetary values can be used but they should be readjusted for inflation and expressed at current prices. Alternatively, the figures could be converted to an index. The steps of time over which the forecast is made can be as short as days, weeks or months (as in a sales plan) but more often they are in quarters or years.

A forecast can never be absolutely correct, except by coincidence — future events are always uncertain. It is usual, therefore, to qualify a forecast. Different predictions could be given based on different assumptions or there could simply be an upper and lower limit either side of the best estimate. The finished forecast should be supported by a description of the underpinning assumptions and their effect. The method of preparing the forecast should also be described, as readers will react more favourably to something they understand. A simple approach is better than a sophisticated but complex method where the user needs to wrestle with the concepts.

Forecasting methods can be divided into two major types: *objective* methods comprising various statistical approaches and *subjective* methods based on surveys of opinion. Table 11.1 shows the most commonly used forecasting methods and how they are suited to different forecasting periods and applications.

TABLE II.I CLASSIFICATION OF FORECASTING METHODS BY APPLICATION

Classification of forecasting method	Period	Application
Objective methods		
Trend projection		
Historical analogy	Medium- to long-term	New products; products susceptible to change
Moving averages	Short- to medium-term	Established products with a recognisable cycle
Exponential smoothing	Short-term	Products which are changing and entering uncharted areas
Models		
Correlation	Short- to medium-term	Where products are influenced by factors on which data is available historically and for the forecast period
Subjective methods		
User opinion	Short- to medium-term	Sales forecasts; new products
Expert opinion	Medium- to long-term	Market and industry forecasts

HISTORICAL ANALOGY

History often repeats itself. If the researcher believes that a product will follow a similar pattern to one which is already established and well-documented, the earlier analogous trend becomes a base for predicting the future.

This philosophy lies behind the 'product life cycle' which argues that most products face recognisable stages of youth, maturity and decline. Identifying the position of a product at any one point in time in its life is critical, as it enables the researcher to predict future sales and, if necessary, rejuvenate or replace the product. The time span from youth to old age could cover 20 or more years and within that period, product modifications distort the smooth lines of the time curve. Interference with the curve is created by economical cycles, legislation and social changes so that it is sometimes difficult to make practical use of the product cycle, even though theoretically it is a useful concept.

Nevertheless, while it may be difficult to plot an entire life cycle for a product, it may be possible to recognise short sections of it. A product launched in America or continental Europe may set a trend which can be expected in the UK a short while later. However, allowance must be made for cultural and economic differences: product launches which have proved successful in Europe cannot necessarily be expected to be repeated in developing nations.

MOVING AVERAGES

One of the simplest methods of obtaining a view of the future is to plot an historical series of data and allow the eye to project the trend forward. Moving averages perform this feat mathematically and therefore accurately and objectively. The projection by eye may be close to reality over the short term but mathematical prediction will provide a good forecast for up to two years ahead. Moving averages smooth the peaks and troughs in the data, creating a trend line which cuts the centre of the figures. (See also Chapter 13.)

Moving averages are a suitable method for predicting from a series of data which has shown regular historical patterns and where there is a long series. Thus they are a suitable means of predicting seasonal sales and those with an evident cycle. They are not suitable for predicting events in rapidly changing markets, where there is a short time series of data or where account has to be taken of a recent major event (such as a new government imposing strong fiscal measures).

EXPONENTIAL SMOOTHING

Predictions using moving averages assume that history, no matter how distant, has an effect on the future equal to that of the most recent past. Often, however, it is recent events which provide the greatest clue to future activity. Exponential smoothing is a mathematical approach which applies such weights. Like all methods of trend projection, it relies on a long series of data, but here five years is probably sufficient, compared with the ten or more years necessary in moving averages. Where such lengthy historical series are not available, the forecast may have to be calculated on quarterly figures, accepting the fact that the forecasting horizon will be that much shorter.

Exponential smoothing is most suited to series of data where there have been no wild fluctuations but a steady growth of decline which is accelerating or decelerating.

CORRELATION

Correlation is a statistical technique for demonstrating the relationship between two series of data. One set of data is known as the *dependent variable* and is the item to be forecast; the other is known as the *independent variable* and is the factor which explains the movement in the dependant variable. The influence of one factor on another is very often obvious:

■   sales of petrol and miles driven

■   steel consumption and car production

■   welding rods and CO_2.

The first test of the existence of any relationship is to plot the two sets of data on a graph to establish visually if the fluctuations appear sympathetic. That they may prove to be so is not, of course, proof of a direct causal relationship. Steel consumption and car production may rise and fall in sympathy — not because cars are the major outlet for steel but because car production is a fair barometer of the country's economic prosperity and it is in this connection that a relationship is apparent. Similarly, historical relationships can change. Cars have become increasingly reliable in recent years and this has resulted in some changes to the relationship between car servicing expenditure and miles driven.

Establishing a strong relationship between two sets of data is the first step in using correlation to arrive at a forecast. To make use of that relationship and predict the future depends upon the availability of a forecast for the independent variable. The accuracy of the forecast of the dependent variable is not only affected by the level of correlation but also by the accuracy of the forecast of the independent variable. Thus there is no point demonstrating a relationship between welding rod sales and CO_2 consumption unless an apparently reliable forecast of CO_2 consumption is readily available over the period of the forecast.

Sometimes an independent variable can be identified which leads the dependent variable. Flat roofs being constructed today can be used to predict sales of the replacement roofing felts market in ten years' time — the life of the original felt. Bad winters influence the sale of road-making machinery six months later when it is needed to repair the ravages of the weather.

For many products, no single independent variable explains the relationship. Fork lift truck demand is not only influenced by GDP, but also by interest rates (which affect the propensity to buy equipment). When more than one independent variable is built into a formula to establish the coefficient of the correlation, the statistical technique is known as *multiple regression*.

The validity of a forecast based on correlation depends on the accuracy of the forecast of the independent variable and the maintenance of the proven relationship into the future. A relationship which has held good for the past ten years may well change over the next five. This means that regression forecasting is best restricted to short- to medium-term horizons.

SURVEYS OF USER OPINIONS

A traditional approach used by market researchers to determine future trends is to ask users how they foresee their consumption of a product or service changing. The 'man in the street' is likely to have more difficulty seeing far into the future than buyers in industry because as high street consumers we tend to react to the products we are presented with and do not dwell on what we will be buying or using in years to come. Even the professional buyer in industry struggles nowadays to see more than a few months into the future, such are the uncertainties of the economy.

Producing *market forecasts* from buyers' claimed intentions is notoriously unreliable for two important reasons. First, buyers are the wrong people to predict the future prospects within a company. They react to demands from production who in turn respond to orders generated by sales. It is the sales and marketing departments who have a better feel for the future though they, too, are not without a bias. Secondly, buyers, like most other employees of a company, lean towards optimism rather than pessimism. It is reasonable that most respondents, if unsure of the future for the company, will incline towards a favourable view out of wishful thinking. It is a brave and rare man who will predict that a company's purchases will fall to zero next year because the company is heading for liquidation — and yet many are.

In constructing a sales forecast for a company it becomes necessary to take account of user opinion, especially that of current customers, and by this we mean the first line customer such as the wholesalers, retailers or the other businesses which buy the products. (In the general scheme of things, few companies supply direct to the public.) Obtaining a prediction of likely purchases from a buyer at a company provides at least one important input for the sales forecast and it also acts as a tacit business commitment.

End users are noted for seeing the future in isolation. Respondents who represent businesses are dismissive of competitors and highly reactive to recent events. A few good weeks' sales and a bullish report on the economy can persuade a respondent that the next two years' prospects are rosy. Similarly, gloomy media reports can talk respondents into a recession. Researchers must not be afraid of tempering end users' opinions. Indeed, it can be better for the researcher to explore the environment which influences a company and then arrive at an independent prediction rather than relying on the users' views. In a business-to-business survey on trends the researcher could, for example, lead the respondent through a series of background questions which are factual:

■ What were the trends in sales over the past year/two years/ three years?

■ To what extent were those increases or decreases in sales due to changes in demand for the products made by the company as opposed other changes such as those brought about by legislation or technology?

■ What changes will be made to the company's products or the method of manufacture over the next year?

This data, backed up by the researcher's knowledge of trends in the end-user markets and changing competition, could enable an informed prediction. However, it should be remembered that a subjective forecast is an expression of individual opinion. It could actually be a better forecast than one derived from a statistical model but the assumptions on which it has been based should be made absolutely clear at the time of reporting.

SURVEYS OF EXPERT OPINION

Very often in business-to-business markets there are no statistical series to develop a trend forecast, or a rapid change in the business environment may make such an approach doubtful in any case. The industrial company may be in a business which is concerned with the tendering for, and therefore the forecast sale of, high-cost single items of plant. The lumpy nature of such demand can lead to large fluctuations in demand depending on when and how the contracts fall.

In such markets the researcher cannot rely on statistical series or the narrow perspective held by buyers and has, therefore, to turn to experts. Expert opinion can be obtained from a variety of sources. Competitors may be prepared to talk in broad terms about the future of the total market, and it would be very difficult for them to concoct their answers if they were asked to justify their statements at every point in the discussion. Also the researcher, with the benefit of other person's views already collected, will be quickly able to spot the deviant. Journalists, university researchers, government officials, suppliers, customers' customers; all may be worth canvassing for their forecasts. There is no single right way to collect the information, as all the methods have their own advantages and disadvantages. Brainstorming sessions are useful in stimulating ideas but the inarticulate suffer while the outspoken may dominate. Also, it can be impractical difficult getting scattered respondents together at the same time.

Depth interviewing is the usual approach. *Delphi interviewing*, in which individuals' views are collected separately and the findings circulated for modified comment, can provide longer term trends but, through exposing the thoughts of others, it may cause some of the less confident contributors to be unduly influenced — possibly incorrectly.

COMPOSITE FORECASTS

A forecast should not necessarily be derived from a single approach. It can be enlightening to compare forecasts arrived at by different techniques. Forecasts should be justifiable and so, where they do not agree, the rationalisation process may uncover flaws which help towards a deeper understanding of market trends.

Long-term forecasting is more difficult now than it has ever been. Uncertainty surrounds the supply of oil and many other raw materials, and for the first time a practical awareness is growing of the problems of robbing the world of irreplaceable resources. Secondly, nations are faced with economic pressures which they do not know how to control. Inflation, recession, interest rates and unemployment affect every supplier of industrial goods and, because their interaction is not fully understood, it is not possible to know how deeply recessions will bite or how long they will last. Thirdly, the world is in a state of fragile political tension in which there is always a possibility of localised wars flaring up to become international incidents. If such events are thought possible or even likely, should they be built into a forecast and, realistically, how could this be done?

The difficulties which beset long-term forecasting pose an important problem to market researchers. Despite the difficulties, market researchers may still be required to advise on opportunities which could involve laying down new plant, employing labour, entering new markets or developing new products. Without a long-term forecast it is not possible to make provision for resources, since the lead time on commissioning a new plant and tooling might be between two and four years. Unfortunately, there is no simple answer — indeed the best solution is to use as many forecasting approaches as possible to cross-check the findings.

12

CORRELATION

■

ESTABLISHING THE RELATIONSHIP BETWEEN TWO VARIABLES

When people drive more miles they use more petrol and their brake linings need replacing more frequently. When temperatures drop we buy overcoats and when temperatures rise sufficiently, we eat ice cream. There are many areas where we can recognise a close link between two factors and see that one is a principal influence on the other. The factors which we examine are known as *variables* and it is extremely useful to researchers to know that if one variable moves so far in a certain direction then the other will also move by a predictable amount. If when it rains people buy more umbrellas, then umbrella manufacturers can plot the wet months and predict their periods of heaviest sales. Since both rainfall and umbrellas increase in tandem we say that the relationship (or correlation, as we prefer to call it) is *positive*. Of course, the movement of the variables may not always be in the same direction. As interest rates increase, so house sales fall. In this case we would say that the correlation is *negative*.

The simplest way of looking at the relationship between two variables is to plot one against the other on a graph. However, just because two variables move in a predictable direction (either positively or negatively) does not mean to say that there is a causal relationship — that is one is dependent on the other. For example, sales of new cars and sales of houses may be closely correlated but this is not the result of any interdependence. Both are at the mercy of economic gloom or boom.

When a relationship is shown to exist between two variables it is important to know which affects which. Spare part sales are dependent on the age of cars; sales of some products are dependent on their price. Spare parts and product sales are *dependent* variables while cars and price are *independent* variables.

Knowledge that a relationship exists between two sets of data can be used by the researcher to predict a figure. Of course, we require data on the independent variable and there is always a fear that this itself could be unreliable. For example, say we knew that the tonnes of steel sold in the UK closely correlated with the gross domestic product (GDP), we could use this knowledge to forecast the market size for steel only if we were confident that we knew exactly what was going to happen to GDP — and this is quite difficult in these uncertain times.

Sometimes there is a lagged relationship between dependent and independent variables which allows a more accurate prediction. The number of planning applications passed by a local authority will, for example, be associated with the level of sales of building materials in that locality; but the latter would lag behind the former by a period of six to twelve months.

Examples of variables which would be expected to have an inter-dependent relationship are:

■   sales of a product and the weather (ice cream and temperature; umbrellas and rain);

■   sales of a product and its price;

■   product sales and advertising expenditure;

■   sales of spare parts and the sales of the original equipment products;

■   the age of a car and its value;

■   the oil price and the reserves of oil;

■   sales of fork-lift trucks and the index of industrial production.

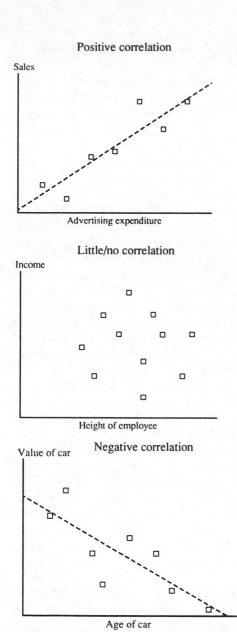

Figure 12.1 Scatter graphs of correlation coefficients

THE COEFFICIENT OF CORRELATION

The degree to which these variables are dependent on each other differs and can be expressed as a measure known as the *coefficient of correlation*. Correlation (ie the relationship) can be positive, negative or zero and, in the first instance, can be tested in a scatter graph. In the examples of scatter graphs shown in Figure 12.1 we can see marks which plot the measurements between two sets of data. So, for example, in the case of product sales and advertising expenditure, the lower the advertising expenditure, the lower the sales and the higher the expenditure the higher the sales. The distribution of the points on the graph shows a pattern which moves upwards from left to right and they cluster around a line which can be drawn between them so that it is the 'best fit' possible.

These scatter graphs can be used for making estimations, using the line to show where to read the sales figure for a given amount of advertising expenditure. Where the points are randomly scattered and there is no evidence of clustering along an axis, then it is not possible to fit a line, there is no relationship between the variables and the data cannot be used for predictive purposes.

The correlation coefficient is a number which falls between +1 and −1 depending on the strength of the relationship between the two variables. The +1 figure indicates a very strong positive relationship and the −1 figure shows a wholly dependent negative link. When there is perfect correlation between two variables it is extremely useful to researchers as the knowledge of what is happening to one of our measurements can enable us with certainty to predict what is happening to the other. Perfect correlation seldom happens in business and the most we can hope for is an indication that the link is very strong. There is no magic figure at which we can say that the correlation is sufficient to enable us to use the relationship for predictive purposes but most statisticians would say that coefficients of more than ± 0.6 are fairly strong.

REGRESSION LINES

We can get a feel for the trend line in a scatter graph by eye but its position derived in this way will only be an approximation. A line of best fit can be drawn mathematically and is called a *regression line*. The purpose in calculating a regression line is to remove judgement and, therefore, human error from the fitting of the trend line. With an accurate trend line a more reliable estimate can be made of one variable from another. For example, a researcher could calculate the best estimate of an advertising appropriation to achieve a certain sales target or he could predict sales of a product with a broad base of demand (eg fork-lift trucks) from a published forecast of the index of industrial production.

The equation which describes a straight line in any graph is:

$$y = a + bx$$

where:

y = the dependent variable
x = the independent variable
a and b = constants which are calculated from the following formulae:

$$b = \frac{\sum xy - \bar{x}\sum y}{\sum x^2 - \bar{x}\sum x}$$

$$a = \bar{y} - b\bar{x}$$

in which y and x are the dependent variable and independent variable as before and:

$$\bar{x} = \textit{average of the x values}$$
$$\bar{y} = \textit{average of y values}$$

The following example illustrates the application of these formulae using sales of photocopiers by a company and its advertising over a five year period. The data is presented in Table 12.1.

TABLE 12.1 COMPANY SALES OF PHOTOCOPIERS AND ASSOCIATED ADVERTISING EXPENDITURE

Year	Sales* (£m)	Advertising expenditure (£000s)	Computed values		
	y	x	xy	x^2	y^2
1988	0.6	20	12	400	0.36
1989	1.0	50	50	2500	1.00
1990	1.2	55	66	3025	1.44
1991	1.4	70	98	4900	1.96
1992	1.4	65	91	4225	1.96
Totals	$\sum y = 5.6$	$\sum x = 260$	$\sum xy = 317$	$\sum x^2 = 15050$	$\sum y^2 = 6.72$
Averages	$\bar{y} = 1.12$	$\bar{x} = 52$			

*All sales figures are adjusted to 1992 prices.

Substituting the derived totals and averages in the equations we get:

$$b = \frac{317 - 52\,(5.6)}{15050 - 52\,(260)}$$

$$= \frac{317 - 291.20}{15050 - 13520}$$

$$= \frac{25.8}{1530}$$

$$b = 0.01686$$
$$a = 1.12 - 0.01686\ (52)$$
$$a = 1.12 - 0.8767$$
$$a = 0.2433$$

The regression line of y on x is therefore:

$$y = a + bx$$
$$y = 0.2433 + 0.0169x$$

Thus the formula can be used to insert values of x (ie advertising expenditure) to determine y (sales of photocopiers) for any future marketing campaign.

The marketing director may wish to know what sales target would be a reasonable expectation by doubling his last year's advertising appropriation to £130 000.

$$y = 0.2433 + 0.0169 \times 130$$
$$y = 0.2433 + 2.197$$
$$y = 2.44\ \text{million}$$

Therefore the best estimate of sales with an advertising appropriation of £130 000 is £2.4 million.

A 'health warning' should perhaps be attached to this type of extrapolation of x values beyond the range on which the regression equation was calculated. Certainly the researcher should be wary of such predictions and the approach could be used with more confidence if it was restricted to interpolating the unmeasured values of x within the range.

CALCULATING THE CORRELATION COEFFICIENT

The coefficient of correlation or r is a measure which helps the market researcher assess how close a relationship is between two variables. The closer the measure is to ± 1.0, the greater the level of sympathy between the two variables. As we have said, anything in excess of 0.6 suggests a reasonable degree of sympathy. However, a value of 0.8 for r does not mean that a relationship is twice as close as a set of data producing a coefficient of 0.4: in fact 0.8 is much closer.

The formula for calculating the coefficient of correlation is expressed as follows:

$$r = \frac{n\sum xy - (\sum x)(\sum y)}{\sqrt{[n\sum x^2 - (\sum x)^2][n\sum y^2 - (\sum y)^2]}}$$

All the terms, with the exception of n, arc as explained earlier.

$$n = \textit{Number of pairs of values}$$

From the example of regression the value of each term can be derived.

$$n = 5$$
$$\sum xy = 317$$
$$\sum x = 260$$
$$\sum y = 5.6$$
$$\sum x^2 = 15050$$
$$\sum y^2 = 6.72$$

Therefore $r =$

$$\frac{5(317) - (260)(5.6)}{\sqrt{[5(15050) - (260)^2][5(6.72) - (5.6)^2]}}$$

$$= \frac{1585 - 1456}{\sqrt{[75250 - 67600][33.6 - 31.36]}}$$

$$= \frac{129}{\sqrt{7650 \times 2.24}}$$

$$= \frac{129}{130.905}$$

$$r = 0.985$$

A very close association indeed.

13

TIME SERIES ANALYSIS

■

THE APPLICATION OF TIME SERIES ANALYSIS

Market researchers are constantly examining data recorded over periods which could be weekly, monthly, quarterly, annually or whatever. This numerical data is generally referred to as *time series*.

By plotting the data graphically the researcher may identify trends or cycles and by eye these can be projected to produce a forecast. Because a result derived in such a way would be subject to errors of judgement, the trend or cycle is fitted mathematically. Figure 13.1 shows a time series of a company's sales over time.

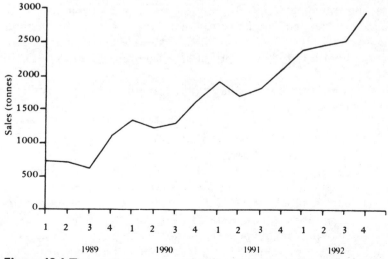

Figure 13.1 Time series — quarterly sales of ABC company 1989–1992

An examination of this graph suggests two important features which help in the understanding of future events.

1. **A trend**: This is the long-term movement in sales which is steadily upwards year by year despite periodic fluctuations.
2. **Seasonal variations:** These are easy to recognise and show a generally poor second and third quarter and a good first and fourth quarter. Furthermore, there are some fluctuations in the curve which show no pattern at all. Cyclical changes, although difficult to recognise and anticipate, could be superimposed on the overall trend.

Beyond these fundamental influences on the trend there could be others. Unforeseen events can always knock a trend off its course and there are many examples of legislation giving a market both an unforeseen boost or killing it dead overnight. Similarly war, fires, floods and catastrophes can affect the overall trend.

CALCULATING THE MOVING AVERAGE

The researcher is most concerned with the two elements which can be anticipated, namely trend and seasonal variations. These can be calculated by the method of *moving averages*. This method is best explained by means of an example. The data used to graph Figure 13.1 is shown in the sales column of figures in Table 13.1.

The procedure for calculating the moving averages, trend and fluctuations, is in five steps:

1. Ensure that the sales data do not include the effect of inflation and that all periods are compatible.
2. Select a number of consecutive periods (in the table we have four quarters) and add them to arrive at an annual total. It should be noted that the choice of number of periods depends on the periodicity of fluctuations. This is usually evident from the peaks and troughs on graphed data. If the number of values chosen is four, then the first four figures are added (quarters one to four in 1989), then the next four

TABLE 13.1 CALCULATION OF MOVING AVERAGES FOR ABC COMPANY 1989-1992
(all figures in tonnes)

Year	Qtr	Sales	Moving annual total	Centred total	Trend	Fluctuations from the trend
1989	1	741			n/a	n/a
	2	721			n/a	n/a
	3	623	3187	7017	877	−254
	4	1102	3830	8182	1023	+79
1990	1	1384	4352	9337	1167	+217
	2	1243	4985	10491	1311	−68
	3	1256	5506	11569	1446	−190
	4	1623	6063	12657	1582	+41
1991	1	1941	6594	13756	1719	+222
	2	1774	7162	14829	1854	−80
	3	1824	7667	15810	1976	−152
	4	2128	8143	16959	2120	+8
1992	1	2417	8816	18313	2289	+128
	2	2447	9497	19745	2468	−21
	3	2505	10248			
	4	2879				

    figures (quarter two in 1989 inclusive to quarter one in 1990).

3.   Add each consecutive pair of moving annual totals to arrive at a centred total.
4.   Divide the centred total by eight to determine the trend.
5.   The difference between the actual values (column one) and the trend (column two) gives the fluctuations from the trend for each quarter.

CALCULATING SEASONAL VARIATIONS

The trend line can now be plotted graphically and extrapolated to obtain a base line forecast. However, a more accurate forecast needs to take account of the seasonal fluctuations. A prediction of these variations can be derived by:

1. averaging the fluctuations from the trend for like quarters.
2. finding their average.
3. subtracting or adding this figure to adjust the seasonal variation (see Table 13.2).

The trend line can be projected by adding 179 tonnes (the latest trend increase computed by subtracting 2289 from 2468) to each previous trend figure, ie quarter three trend = 2468 + 179 = 2647; quarter four trend = 2647 + 179 = 2826 etc).

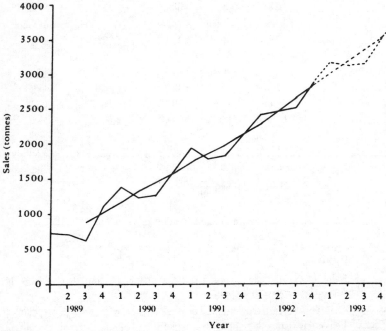

Figure 13.2 Forecast quarterly sales and trends of ABC company 1989–1993

TABLE 13.2 ESTABLISHING SEASONAL VARIATION

Year	Quarter			
	1	2	3	4
1989			−254	+79
1990	+217	−68	−190	+41
1991	+222	−80	−152	+8
1992	+128	−21		
Total	+567	−169	−596	+128
Average (÷3)	+189	−56	−199	+43
Adjustment for seasonality*	+6	+6	+6	+6
Seasonal variation	+195	−50	−193	+49

*Adjustment for seasonality derived by taking the averages and:
$$+189$$
$$-56$$
$$-199$$
$$+43$$
$$\overline{-23}$$
$$-23 \div 4 = -5.75, say\ 6$$

By plotting the seasonal variations either side of the trend line, a forecast can be achieved for forthcoming periods (see Figure 13.2).

This approach is suitable for short-term forecasts of, say, four quarters where the seasonality is fairly regular. It cannot cope with wild fluctuations of data nor does it take sufficient account of any strong, recent trend since this type of effect is dampened by averaging with other figures.

BIBLIOGRAPHY

∎

STATISTICS

Alt, Mick (1990) *Exploring Hyperspace: A Non-mathematical Explanation of Multivariate Analysis*, McGraw-Hill, Maidenhead

Cochran, W G (1977) *Sampling Techniques* (3rd edition), John Wiley, Chichester

Gilchrist, Warren (1984) *Statistical Forecasting*, John Wiley & Sons, Chichester

Kish, L (1965) *Survey Sampling*, John Wiley, Chichester

Moroney, M J (1953) *Facts From Figures*, Pelican, London

Stuart (1976) *Basic Ideas of Scientific Sampling* (2nd edition), Edward Arnold (formally Griffin), Sevenoaks

Thirlkettle, G L (1981) *Wheldon's Business Statistics and Statistical Method*, Macdonald & Evans, Plymouth

GENERAL READING ON MARKET RESEARCH (CONSUMER RESEARCH ORIENTATED)

Aaker, David A & Day, George S (1990) *Marketing Research*, John Wiley, Chichester

Baker, Michael J (1991) *Research for Marketing*, Macmillan, London

Birn, R, Hague, P & Vangelder, P (Eds) (1990) *A Handbook of Market Research Techniques*, Kogan Page, London

Birn, Robin (1991) *The Effective Use of Market Research*, Kogan Page, London

Cannon, Tom (1973) *Advertising Research*, Intertext, Aylesbury

Chisnall, Peter (1991) *The Essence of Marketing Research*, Prentice-Hall, Englewood Cliffs, New Jersey

Chisnall, Peter (1992) *Marketing Research*, McGraw-Hill, Maidenhead

Crimp, Margaret (1990) *The Marketing Research Process*, Prentice-Hall, Englewood Cliffs, New Jersey

Crouch, S (1984) *Marketing Research for Managers,* Heinemann, Oxford

Ehrenberg, A S C (1988) *Repeat Buying*, Edward Arnold, Sevenoaks

Gordon, Wendy & Langmaid, Roy (1988) *Qualitative Market Research*, Gower, Aldershot

Gorton, Keith & Doole, Isobel (1989) *Low-Cost Marketing Research*, John Wiley & Sons, Chichester

Green, P & Tull, J (1978) *Research for Marketing Decisions*, Prentice-Hall, Englewood Cliffs, New Jersey

Hague, Paul N & Jackson, Peter (1987) *Do Your Own Market Research*, Kogan Page, London

Hague, Paul N & Jackson, Peter (1990) *How to Do Marketing Research*, Kogan Page, London

Hague, Paul (1993) *Interviewing*, Kogan Page, London

Jain, A K, Pinson, P & Ratchford, B (1982) *Marketing Research – Applications and Problems*, John Wiley & Sons, Chichester

Kreuger, Richard A (1989) *Focus Groups (A Practical Guide for Small Businesses)*, Sage Publications, London

Robson, S & Foster, A (Eds) (1989) *Qualitative Research in Action*, Edward Arnold, Sevenoaks

Talmage, P A (1988) *Dictionary of Marketing Research*, Market Research Society, London

Walker, R (Ed) (1985) *Applied Qualitative Research*, Gower, Aldershot

Williams, Keith (1981) *Behavioural Aspects of Marketing*, Heinemann, Oxford

Worcester, R M & Downham, J (Eds) (1986) *Consumer Market Research Handbook*, Elsevier, Netherlands

GENERAL READING ON INDUSTRIAL MARKET RESEARCH

Hague, Paul N & Jackson, Peter (1992) *Marketing Research in Practice*, Kogan Page, London

MacLean, Ian (Ed.) (1976) *Handbook of Industrial Marketing Research*, Kluwer-Harrap, Brentford

Stacey, N A H & Wilson, Aubrey (1963) *Industrial Market Research – Management Techniques*, Hutchinson, London

Sutherland, Ken (Ed) (1991) *Researching Business Markets*, Kogan Page (in association with the Industrial Marketing Research Association), London

Wilson, Aubrey (1968) *The Assessment of Industrial Markets*, Hutchinson, London

QUESTIONNAIRES

Hague, Paul (1993) *Questionnaire Design*, Kogan Page, London

Oppenheim, A N (1970) *Questionnaire Design and Attitude Measurement*, Heinemann, Oxford

Wolfe, A (1984) *Standardised Questions*, Market Research Society, London

PRESENTATIONS AND REPORT WRITING

Jay, Anthony (1976) *Slide Rules*, Video Arts, London

May, John (1982) *How to Make Effective Business Presentations*, McGraw-Hill, Maidenhead

JOURNALS AND PERIODICALS

Business Marketing Digest, (formally Industrial Marketing Digest), quarterly, Wallington, Surrey

Harvard Business Review, bi-monthly, Boston, Massachusetts

Journal of The Market Research Society, quarterly, London

Marketing, weekly, London

OTHER READING MATERIAL

Conference papers published every year by the Market Research Society and the Industrial Marketing Research Association.

INDEX

■